GW00498628

ARSENAL FOOTBALL CLUB

Founded: 1886
Colours: Red shirts with white sleeves, white shorts
Ground: Arsenal Stadium, Highbury, London N5
Telephone: 01-226 0304
Ground Capacity: 60,000
Record Attendance: 73,295 v Sunderland, First Division, 9 March 1935
Record Receipts: £116,498 v Juventus, Cup-winners' Cup semi-final,
   9 April 1980
Pitch measurement: 110 yards by 71 yards
Honours: First Division Champions 1930-1, 1932-3, 1933-4, 1934-5,
   1937-8, 1947-8, 1952-3, 1970-1; Runners-up 1925-6, 1931-2,
   1972-3. Second Division Runners-up 1903-4. FA Cup Winners
   1929-30, 1935-6, 1949-50, 1970-1, 1978-9; Runners-up 1926-7,
   1931-2, 1951-2, 1971-2, 1977-8, 1979-80. Football League Cup
   Runners-up 1967-8, 1968-9. European Fairs Cup Winners 1969-70.
   European Cup-winners' Cup Runners-up 1979-80.
Record Win: 12-0 v Loughborough Town, Second Division,
   12 March 1900
Record Defeat: 0-8 v Loughborough Town, Second Division,
   12 December 1896
Most League Points gained: 66, First Division, 1930-1
Most League Goals Scored: 127, First Division, 1930-1
Highest League Scorer in a Season: Ted Drake, 42, First Division
   1934-5
Most League Goals in Aggregate Total: Cliff Bastin, 150, 1930-47
Most League Appearances: 500, George Armstrong, 1960-77
Managers since World War II: George Allison, Tom Whittaker,
   Jack Crayston, George Swindin, Billy Wright, Bertie Mee,
   Terry Neill
How to reach Highbury: Arsenal Underground station (Piccadilly Line)
   is one minute's walk from ground. Drayton Park (Northern Line) and
   Finsbury Park (Piccadilly & Victoria) also within walking distance.
   Buses 4A, 19, 106, 141A, 236
Club Shop is on the ground

*(Overleaf) The Wembley trail. Swansea's full-back
Keane tips the ball over the bar and from the penalty
Wally Barnes scores Arsenal's second goal in their
fourth round FA Cup tie at Highbury, January 1950.*

*(Opposite) Another historic moment. The Graf
Zeppelin over Wembley during the 1930 FA Cup final
against Huddersfield.*

The Story of
ARSENAL

Anton Rippon

ISBN 0 86190 023 5

Typeset by Hemmings Ltd, Leicester.
Printed in Great Britain by
Butler & Tanner Ltd, Frome, for
Moorland Publishing Company Ltd,
PO Box 2, 9-11 Station Street, Ashbourne,
Derbyshire, DE6 1DZ, England

1886-1951

Whenever the name of Arsenal Football Club is mentioned, one feels obliged to stand up. For over fifty years it has been one of the most revered in the world-wide game. From the streets of Islington to the beaches of Copacabana, small boys have kicked a ball about and imagined themselves to be wearing the famous red and white shirts of Arsenal. As that most distinguished of soccer writers, Geoffrey Green, once wrote about the name, 'It is a royal salute by gunfire.'

This adulation with which all football holds the club from Highbury, London N5, stems from the 1930s when a man called Herbert Chapman arrived at Arsenal Stadium and set the club on the road to becoming one of the greatest—if not *the* greatest—in the game. That period between the wars ensured that Arsenal would forever be the aristocrats of football. And Arsenal supporters can be forgiven for thinking that their club has a divine right to success.

But this is not the case. Until Chapman came on the scene, Arsenal had been a very ordinary club. Indeed, for some of its early career, the very future of the club had been in doubt; and it is important to remember this. To forget it would be to dismiss without a second thought the dedication, hardwork and foresight of those early Gunners who laid the foundations upon which the great Chapman was to build the Arsenal empire.

Without these pioneers, Arsenal fans of later years would never have known the epic Championship sides and Cup-winning teams of the 1930s; nor the glorious 'Double' winners of 1971; nor the side which reached three FA Cup finals in three years at the end of the 1970s and the beginning of the 1980s. Without them, there would be no Arsenal—and football would be much the poorer.

In the 1880s, football was at a low ebb, particularly in the south where the opposition to professionalism—legalised in the north in 1885—meant that people were turning away from the game. Also, the south's supremacy with teams like Old Etonians, Wanderers, Royal Engineers, Clapham, and the Oxford and Cambridge teams, was at an end. Teams like Blackburn Olympic, Blackburn Rovers, Aston Villa, Notts County and West Brom held the stage. For most southerners, the game of Rugby began to have more appeal.

But there were still pockets of soccer resistance held mainly by men from the north who refused to let go of their Association game when coming south to find work. One such pocket was at the Woolwich Arsenal where, in 1886, a football club was formed. The men worked in the Dial Square section of the great munition works and they already had a cricket team. Already a man called Joseph Smith had made an abortive attempt to start a soccer club. Now a second attempt was made—and this time it succeeded.

Three men could claim football's eternal gratitude for re-lighting the embers that became the undying flame of Arsenal. David Danskin, a Scotsman from Kirkcaldy, Fred Beardsley, who had played in goal for Nottingham Forest, and Richard Pearce, from Bolton, had all come south to work at the munition works. According to the club's first secretary, George 'Elijah' Watkins, writing in *Football Chat and Athletic World* in 1902, Arsenal was formed as Dial Square FC at a meeting at the Prince of Wales public house at Plumstead Common in October 1886.

A subscription list was started and 5s 6d collected towards a ball. Danskin added 5s of his own money and the new club bought its ball and had 1s 3d change to put into the bank. Thus, the financial affairs of the earliest Arsenal club were conducted along lines of great economy! That early team must have been a sight to behold. The players were responsible for their own kit and each wore a different coloured shirt. Richard Pearce, for instance, favoured a shirt of blue and black hoops with long trousers cut down to make shorts and ordinary shoes with metal bars nailed across the soles.

Dial Square's first match was against the well-known Eastern Wanderers at Millwall sometime before Christmas 1886. Mr Watkins remembered, 'The ground was bounded by back-yards about two-thirds of the area, and the other portion was

---

The team for that first-ever game against Eastern Wanderers at Millwall in 1886-7 was: Beardsley, Danskin (capt), Porteous, Gregory, Bee, Wolfe, Smith, Moy, Whitehead, Morris, Duggan.
For the first home game, against Erith at Plumstead Common on 8 January 1887, Arsenal fielded the following line-up: Beardsley, Danskin, Porteous, Gregory, Price, Wells, Smith, Moy, Whitehead, Crighton, Bee.

either a ditch or a sewer.' Whatever the conditions, Dial Square must have relished the fact that they won their first match 6-0.

Interest was now growing and besides Beardsley, the new club attracted more players who had been with Nottingham Forest. In December 1886, a meeting was held at the Royal Oak Hotel in Plumstead and it was decided that the name Dial Square was too narrow a title for a club which now represented the whole works. It was resolved that, henceforward, the club should be called Royal Arsenal. When the subject of club colours came up for discussion, it was resolved that, as some of the ex-Forest men still had their red shirts, the colours of the new club should also be red. At some stage in those early days it appears that Beardsley wrote to Forest and asked for more shirts. He received a complete new strip, a gift which would have been especially welcome to a struggling new club.

On 8 January 1887, Arsenal played what is generally regarded as their first home match when they met Erith on Plumstead Common. Other games followed and at the end of that first season, Arsenal's record read: Played 10, Won 7, Drawn 2, Lost 1, Goals for 36, Goals against 8. In their second season (1887-8) Arsenal moved to the Sportsman Ground, owned by Mr Walton, a pig-breeder, where they staged an Oxford v London game. Arsenal reached the second round of the London Senior Cup before losing to the powerful Barnes team and also enjoyed success with matches against Millwall, Rifle Brigade, Erith and Deptford Iona.

In 1888-9 Arsenal were on the move again, this time to the Manor Ground owned by a Mr Cavey, and again the club did well in friendly games. In 1889-90 Arsenal appeared in the FA Cup for the first time and also tasted their first success in competition, lifting the London Charity, Kent Senior and Kent Junior Cups.

Royal Arsenal 1888, then an amateur club. The captain was Arthur Brown, on the left of the three seated players.

That first FA Cup tie was against Lyndhurst at the Manor Ground on 5 October 1889 when Arsenal won the first qualifying round match 11-0. In the next round Arsenal drew 2-2 with the Norfolk club, Thorpe. Thorpe were unable to make the journey to London for the replay and so Arsenal went through to the next round and a 5-2 home win over Crusaders. In their first season in the FA Cup, Arsenal were now within ninety minutes of the competition proper. But in the last qualifying round they were hammered 5-1 at the Manor Ground by Swifts (who themselves were beaten 6-1 at Sheffield Wednesday in the first round proper).

But Arsenal did fare well in three other Cups that season. In the London Charity Cup, Arsenal beat Old Westminsters 3-1 in the final before 10,000 spectators with Fred Beardsley still in goal. J. W. Meggs, who had represented London against Sheffield that season was unfit and his place in the side was taken by W. F. Fry of London Caledonians. In the Kent Senior Cup, Arsenal faced a tough semi-final when they visited Chatham, winners of the trophy for the previous three seasons. But the Gunners hammered them 5-0 and then beat Thanet Wanderers 3-0 in the final, also at Chatham.

Arsenal also reached the final of the London Senior Cup in 1889-90. They beat Unity 4-1, Foxes 4-1, and St Martin's Athletic 6-0 on their way to the semi-finals where Robertson (2) and Horsington scored in the 3-1 win over London Caledonians at the Essex County Ground at Leyton. In the final, Arsenal lost a man injured early in the game and could not hold Old Westminsters who gained revenge for their Charity Cup defeat by winning 1-0. But the season had been an overall success for Arsenal who were declared unofficial 'football champions of the South' by the sporting press.

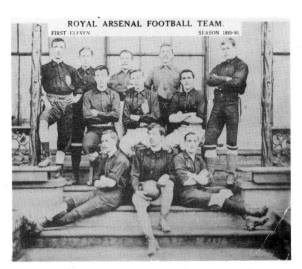

The Royal Arsenal first team 1889-90. Back row, left to right: P. Connolly, J. W. Meggs, F. W. Beardsley, J. McBean, H. R. Robertson. Middle row: D. Howat, J M. Bates, J. W. Julian. Bottom row: R. T. Horsington, H. Barbour, H. Offer. Fred Beardsley is the man eternally credited with founding the Gunners at Woolwich Arsenal. This team won the London Charity Cup and the Kent Senior and Junior Cups.

In 1890-1 Arsenal reached the first round proper of the FA Cup for the first time when they entertained Derby County on 17 January 1891. The game was played at the Invicta Ground, to where Arsenal had made yet another change of home, but Derby won 2-1. In their other Cups, Arsenal lost the three they had won the previous season, including a semi-final defeat in the London Charity Cup when Old Carthusians won a second replay, 2-1 after draws of 1-1 and 2-2. But the London Senior Cup did come to the club when Arsenal pulled back from 2-0 down against Clapton at Kennington Oval and three goals in the last 25 minutes put them through to the final where they crushed St Bartholomew's Hospital 6-0. The *Kentish Independent* commented: 'Excitement is a mild description of the scene in Woolwich and Plumstead on the return of the football champions on Saturday night.'

> *On Easter Monday 1891 Arsenal beat Scottish Cup winners Heart of Midlothian before 12,000 at the Invicta Ground. The following day, 7,000 saw Arsenal beat Nottingham Forest on the same pitch.*

One of the by-products of Arsenal's success was that professional clubs from the North were now casting envious glances at Arsenal's amateur stars and after Derby had won that FA Cup tie in 1891, they offered terms to two Arsenal players, Buist

and Connolly. Arsenal felt that there was only one answer and at the annual meeting at the Windsor Castle Hotel in the summer of 1891, committee man Jack Humble, supported by William B. Jackson, proposed that the club adopt professionalism. The proposal was carried and the professional club was born.

The step was almost suicidal. The southern clubs, shocked and offended by Arsenal's 'defection' to the professional ranks, cast them out. Arsenal were expelled from the London FA and lost almost all their prestigious friendly games. In order to carry on, the club had to arrange games with the Northern and Midland professional clubs. Among the games played were Sheffield United (0-2), West Brom (1-1), Bootle (2-2), Long Eaton Rangers (3-1) and Sheffield Wednesday (1-8 — Arsenal's heaviest defeat up to that time). In addition, Arsenal's hopes of a good FA Cup run came to nothing when they lost 5-1 at Small Heath in the first round proper.

Arsenal's second season as a professional club saw them continue with friendly games against the top clubs north of Birmingham. In the first round proper of the FA Cup they faced a long haul to Sunderland where they were crushed 6-0, and at the end of 1892-3 a dispute arose over the rent of the Invicta Ground. The owners wanted £350 per annum, plus taxes, whereas Arsenal refused to pay more than £300, inclusive of all charges. The result was that Arsenal formed themselves into a limited company with share capital of £4,000 and went back to the Manor Ground which they purchased outright, and which was to be their home until they moved to Highbury in 1913.

But one thing was still lacking and that was a set of permanent fixtures. Arsenal had tried to form a Southern League — at the time without success — and in the close season of 1893 the club made a brave decision. Arsenal applied for the Second Division of the Football League — then just five seasons old — and were accepted along with Liverpool, Middlesbrough Ironopolis, Newcastle and Rotherham. It was a brave decision because Arsenal were the only club south of Birmingham and joining the League meant that they were committed to long and expensive journeys every other week.

Skippered by right-back Powell, Arsenal drew their first-ever Football League match on the opening day of the 1893-4 season. On 2 September 1893 Newcastle United came to the Manor Ground and held their fellow newcomers to a 2-2 scoreline. On a fine, sunny day, Arsenal sped into a 2-0 lead before allowing Newcastle to pull back the goals. One week later, Arsenal played their first away game in the League, losing 3-2 at Trent

Bridge to Notts County. On the following Monday, Walsall were beaten 4-0 at the Manor Ground and then Grimsby came south and were also beaten, 3-1. On the last day of September, Arsenal travelled to Newcastle and provided the opposition for United's first home League match. It was an unhappy day for Arsenal as hat-tricks from United's Wallace and Thompson sank the Gunners 6-0.

Two weeks later, Arsenal started their FA Cup campaign with a resounding 12-0 first qualifying round win over Ashford United. Clapton, Millwall and the 2nd Scots Guards followed before Sheffield Wednesday—by now a First Division side—won 2-1 at the Manor Ground in the first round proper. Arsenal got back to their League programme a week later with a 3-0 defeat at Lincoln and they ended the season on a bleak note by losing their last three games—all at home—to Notts County, Small Heath and Burton Swifts. Arsenal's first season in the Football League ended with them in ninth position.

Arsenal's first decade in the Football League was one of modest success. In their second season they opened with successive defeats at the hands of Lincoln, Grimsby and Burton Swifts, before winning their next seven games. They dropped only three more points at Manor Ground and that defeat by Grimsby turned out to be Arsenal's only home defeat of the season. Away from home, they could not maintain their form and they finished eighth. The highlights of 1895-6 included a 7-0 win over Crewe Alexandra and a 6-0 win over Loughborough Town, newcomers to the Second Division at the expense of Walsall Town Swifts. Arsenal also had good reason to relish the visits of the Burton clubs and they beat Swifts 5-0 and Wanderers 3-0, although losing both games in Staffordshire and eventually finishing seventh.

1896-7 was a notable season in the story of Arsenal by now known as Woolwich Arsenal. First, they finished tenth in Division Two—the club's lowest-ever League position—and they lost 8-0 at Loughborough on 12 December 1896, a result which is still the club's heaviest defeat. In addition, the club failed to reach the competition proper of the FA Cup, although Arsenal Reserves made some amends by taking the Kent County League Championship.

The splendidly-named Caesar A. Llewellyn Jenkyns, signed from Small Heath, became the first Arsenal player to play in an international while at the club when he continued his run in the Wales team; and in 1897-8, Arsenal appointed T. B. Mitchell of Blackburn Rovers as manager, although he was soon replaced by G. Elcoat of Stockton. In 1899-1900 Arsenal had their third

manager in as many seasons when Harry Bradshaw came to the Manor Ground. And it was Bradshaw who guided the side into the First Division.

But before the Gunners made the jump to the top division, they faced crisis off the field. In 1899 the Boer War broke out and besides many Arsenal fans being sent overseas in the army, many more were required to work overtime in the munition factory. Gates inevitably suffered and in 1902-3, funds were so low that the club held an archery tournament to raise money. Over £1,200 was raised and this was spent on strengthening the team which had finished fourth and third respectively in 1901-2 and 1902-3 and which needed new players to push it that little bit further into the top flight.

Bradshaw had started to build his promotion side in 1900-1 when he signed goalkeeper James Ashcroft from Sheppey and defender Cross from Dartford. In 1901-2 Arsenal's defence was so strong that only nine goals were conceded at home, and only twenty-six in all League games. Three successive defeats in December 1902 were enough to deny Arsenal promotion that season, though there was some compensation in the FA Cup when Arsenal's game with Sheffield United—then one of the great English club sides—attracted 25,000 in the first round proper, although the Yorkshiremen spoiled the day for Arsenal by winning 3-1.

In 1903-4 Arsenal won promotion. Halfway through the season it looked as though the Gunners and Preston had turned it into a two-horse race but a late challenge from Manchester United put the issue into doubt right up until the final hurdle. Arsenal needed to draw their last game of the season—at home to Burslem Port Vale on 25 April 1904—and this they did 0-0. Preston won 1-0 at Blackpool five days later to take the Second

Woolwich Arsenal 1904-05. Back row, left to right: R. Drummond (trainer), P. Kelso (manager), A. Gray, J. Ashcroft, J. Grant (director), J. Jackson (captain), J. Bigden, P. Sands, R. M. Dow (Hon. Sec.). Front row: J. Dick, T. Briercliffe, J. Coleman, W. K. Gooing, J. Hunter. J. Satterthwaite, G. Buchan.

JAMES ASHCROFT.

An Edwardian postcard of James Ashcroft, Arsenal's great goalkeeper who played three times for England in 1906.

Division title one point ahead of Arsenal, but the main thing was that the Gunners were now a First Division side. Ashcroft and Gooing played in all thirty-four League games while Shanks was top scorer with twenty-five goals, a feat which earned him an international cap for Ireland against Wales that season.

Arsenal won promotion from the Second Division in 1903-4 for the only time in their history, discounting their elevation for 1919-20. Here is that 1903-4 top three:

	P	W	D	L	F	A	Pts
Preston	*34*	*20*	*10*	*4*	*62*	*24*	*50*
Arsenal	*34*	*21*	*7*	*6*	*91*	*22*	*49*
Manchester Utd	*34*	*20*	*8*	*6*	*65*	*33*	*48*

Before Arsenal could kick a ball in the First Division, Harry Bradshaw surprisingly left for Fulham and his job at the Manor Ground was taken over by Peter Kelso, a Scot from Hibernian. Apart from Bristol City, Arsenal were still the only Football League side south of Birmingham. On 3 September 1904, they played their first-ever First Division game by travelling to Newcastle—who, strangely, had provided Arsenal's first-ever Second Division opposition—and lost 3-0 to goals

from the Magpies' Orr (2) and Rutherford. Newcastle were the only team to do the 'double' over Arsenal that season—winning 2-0 at the Manor Ground on 31 December—and Arsenal finished a reasonable tenth. Shanks again found himself in the Ireland team.

In their second season in the First Division Arsenal progressed past the second round proper of the FA Cup for the first time. In fact, they went all the way to the 1905-6 semi-finals where they met Newcastle, champions and beaten finalists the previous season. Twenty thousand watched the game at Stoke where Newcastle went into their second successive final with a 2-0 win. Arsenal finished twelfth in the table and the following season were back in the semi-finals of the FA Cup again. In fact, this was Arsenal's best season to date.

By 20 October, thanks to a good start in which they dropped only three points in their first nine games, Arsenal headed the table one point ahead of Everton. Only a lean spell in February, when they lost four successive games, cost them the title and they finished 1906-7 in seventh place, seven points behind champions Newcastle. In the FA Cup Arsenal beat Grimsby, Bristol City, Bristol Rovers and Barnsley before Sheffield Wednesday beat them, 3-1 in the semi-final at Birmingham.

In 1907-8, when Arsenal were fourteenth, the club signed a young wing-half from Accrington Stanley. Joe Shaw made only one appearance that season but it was the start of a career which saw him a regular choice in the first team until 1921, by which time he had played in 308 League games, before joining the backroom staff. On the Arsenal staff during Joe Shaw's first season were other names which would become more famous with other clubs, including Andy Ducat, who went to Villa, and Jackie Mordue, who left for Sunderland.

The Gunners were pioneers of foreign tours. This is a rare action shot from Woolwich Arsenal's 5-1 win over Slavia in Prague during the club's tour in 1908. Their visit followed the first official international ever played by England against a foreign country — a 6-1 win over Austria in Vienna on 6 June 1908.

Woolwich Arsenal 1908-09. Back row, left to right: Dick, Greenaway, McEachrane, Curle. Middle row: G. Morrell (manager), Gray, McDonald, Shaw, Ducat, Cross, Raybould, Sands, R. Dunmore (trainer). Front row: Lewis, Satterthwaite, Lee, Neave.

WOOLWICH ARSENAL LEAGUE TEAM, 1908-9.

After their two successive FA Cup semi-finals of 1906 and 1907, Arsenal had to wait until 1926-7 before they reached that stage again. And in the First Division their fortunes began to slump after 1908-9 when they achieved their highest position—sixth—up to that time. Relegation loomed large at Plumstead in 1909-10 when Arsenal missed the drop by two points, finishing narrowly ahead of Chelsea, who went down with Bolton. Arsenal did not gain an away point until 13 November when they drew 1-1 at Sheffield Wednesday; and seven successive defeats gave manager Morrell—who had taken over from Kelso in 1908—some sleepless nights. In the end, Arsenal's last five games produced three wins and two draws. It was enough to give them a stay of execution.

For the next two seasons Arsenal actually enjoyed an improvement in their League fortunes. In 1910-11 Arsenal had to wait until their eighth match for a win. Then, after losing 3-0 to First Division newcomers Oldham Athletic at Oldham on 6 March, Arsenal played their last eleven games without defeat, picking up seventeen points and conceding only three goals. Alf Common, who had found fame by moving from Sunderland to Middlesbrough as the first £1,000 transfer in 1905, moved to Arsenal and scored six goals in twenty-nine games, as well as helping Chalmers to fifteen in the same number. Arsenal finished tenth and began to think that a revival was round the corner.

In 1911-12 Arsenal maintained tenth position but the dark storm clouds were gathering rapidly

Arsenal and Spurs played an exhibition match during the Vienna Festival of 1912. Arsenal won the game, and a silver cup, with players in the side including Peart, Thompson, Winship and Grant. Spurs' side included Billy Minter and Bert Middlemiss.

Woolwich Arsenal 1910-11. Back row, left to right: Hardy (trainer), Dick, Thomas, Bateup, Common, Rippon, Hedley. Middle row: Gray, Ducat, Grant, McDonald, Rogers, Sands. Front row: Lewis, McKinnon, Greenaway, Heppinstall, G. Morrell (manager), Logan, Neave, Shaw, McEachrane. Alf Common, the game's first four-figure transfer deal, was given a free transfer to the Gunners so that hard-up Middlesbrough did not have to pay him a benefit!

and in 1912-13, the club was relegated to the Second Division. It was a disasterous season for Arsenal, finishing bottom with only eighteen points and with only three wins all season. A measure of the club's lack of fire-power is the fact that Randall led the scorers with just four goals—the lowest-ever by a Football League leading scorer. Arsenal beat Sheffield Wednesday 3-1 at Bramall Lane on 21 September 1912. Their next win was on 8 March 1913 when they won 1-0 at Manchester City—a run of twenty-three matches without a win. And the club's bank balance at the end of the season was just £19.

> *Arsenal were relegated for the only time in the club's history in 1912-13. The bottom three places were:*
>
> | | | | | | | | | |
> |---|---|---|---|---|---|---|---|---|
> | 18 | Chelsea | 38 | 11 | 6 | 21 | 51 | 73 | 28 |
> | 19 | Notts County | 38 | 7 | 9 | 22 | 28 | 56 | 23 |
> | 20 | Arsenal | 38 | 3 | 12 | 23 | 26 | 74 | 18 |
>
> *The club's scorers were: Randall 4, Flannagan 3, McLoughlin 3, Burrell 2, Devine 2, Graham 2, Grant 2, Hanks 2, Lewis 2, Duncan 1, Sands 1, Stonley 1, Winship 1.*

A saviour had to be found and he came in the form of a wealthy property dealer, Sir Henry Norris. Immediately he saw that Arsenal needed to move gounds. The Manor Ground at Plumstead was some twenty minutes tram ride beyond the present home of Charlton Athletic. Public transport from the City was poor, and there were now the added competitions of Fulham, Spurs, Clapton Orient and Chelsea, as well as the powerful Southern League clubs, all vying for support.

Sir Henry moved the club ten miles across London to the grounds of a theological college at Highbury. It was the beginning of today's great Arsenal Stadium, although both Spurs and Orient complained about the move, seeing it as a direct threat to their own support.

> *Facilities at Highbury in the early years were primitive. In the first match there, former Newcastle United inside-forward George Jobey had the distinction of scoring the first-ever goal on the famous ground and then being carried off on a milk cart! Jobey injured his ankle and trainer George Hardy borrowed the cart from David Lewis, a dairyman in Gillespie Road, and trundled Jobey back to his lodgings near the ground.*

The Woolwich part of Arsenal's title now became a misnomer and the club became simply 'Arsenal Football Club' for the 1913-14 season. The first game back in the Second Division also saw the first match at Highbury when Leicester Fosse were the visitors on 6 September 1913. Arsenal won 2-1 with goals from George Jobey and Andy Devine (from the penalty spot) and they finished the season in third position, level on points with promoted Bradford, who had a better goal average.

The last season at the Manor Ground. April 1913 and the Gunners, already doomed to relegation, put Mancheter United's goal under pressure. The result was 0-0 and by the start of the following season Arsenal had moved from Plumstead to Highbury and were a Second Division club.

The first season after World War I. Pagnam and Lewis put the Rochdale goalkeeper in some difficulty during the FA Cup third round tie in January 1920. Arsenal beat the non-League side 4-2.

Before the glory . . . Arsenal of 1921, without an international in the team, finished ninth in Division One and were knocked out of the FA Cup at the first hurdle. Back row, left to right: Alf Baker, Joe Shaw, Ernie Williamson, Arthur Hutchins, Angus McKinnon, Chris Buckley. Front row: Bill Smith, Freddie Groves, Ernest Coupland, Frank Bradshaw, Billy Blythe. Straw-hatted in the background is manager Leslie Knighton.

It was a fantastic finish. On the last day of the season Notts County were already assured of promotion but the second spot lay between Arsenal and the Yorkshire club. On 25 April, Arsenal won 2-0 at Glossop, but on the same day, Bradford beat Blackpool 4-1 at home to edge Arsenal out by just 0.09 of a goal. How strange to think that Bradford are no longer members of the Football League, while Arsenal recovered to such greatness.

In October 1913, Arsenal signed John Rutherford, Newcastle United's great right-winger, for £800. Rutherford, aged twenty-nine, had won eleven England caps, three First Division championship medals and an FA Cup-winners' medal with Newcastle. He was to add 233 League appearances with Arsenal to the 292 he had already made with Newcastle, and in 1913-14 he played in twenty-one games and scored six goals.

Sheffield United's goalkeeper John Lievesley signed the same season as Rutherford and other players came in the shape of full-back Benson, also from Sheffield United, and centre-half Buckley from Aston Villa. Manchester City's Scottish inside-forward Billy Blyth joined Arsenal in 1914-15 — the last before football closed down for World War I — and Arsenal finished sixth with only four away wins making their task impossible.

By the time football started again in 1919-20, Arsenal were back in the First Division, though how they did it remains a mystery to this day. The Football League decided to increase the size of the First Division by two clubs and the logical thing to do would have been to retain the bottom two clubs of 1914-15, Chelsea and Spurs. A less obvious move was to promote the Second Division's third

and fourth clubs that season, Barnsley and Wolves. But thanks to some behind-the-scenes lobbying by Sir Henry Norris, it was sixth placed Arsenal who were elected at the expense of Spurs, with Chelsea retaining their place. It took White Hart Lane a long time to forgive Arsenal for looking after themselves in this way.

Back in the First Division Arsenal had, inevitably after the years of war, several new players including Baker, Butler and Hutchins. 'Doughy' Baker, a miner from Ilkeston, was generally regarded as a wing-half but he went on to play in every position except goal for Arsenal, eventually winning an England cap. Jack Butler became a member of the famous half-back line of the 1920s — Baker, Butler and Blyth — and he joined Arsenal from Dartford, though he was born in Colombo.

Full-back Hutchins came from Southern League side Croydon Common — where he was top scorer with seven goals from the penalty spot — and together these players and those who remained from before the war, made up the nucleus of new manager Leslie Knighton's post-war Arsenal eleven. Other players like Pagnam, White, Toner, Williamson and Dunn began to appear in the Arsenal line-up. Left-winger Joe Toner was an Irishman spotted by former Derby winger Toby Mercer and his speed and accurate crossing made him an important part of the Arsenal team in those early years of struggle in the 1920s.

The first six seasons on the resumption of peacetime football brought Arsenal only moderate

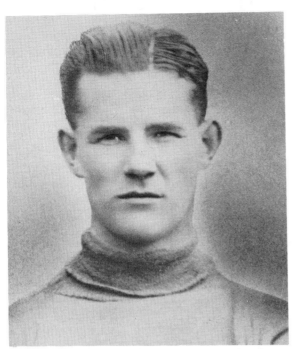

Goalkeeper Ernie Williamson, signed from Croydon Common, who played 105 league games for Arsenal between 1920 and 1923 when he was transferred to Norwich.

success. In the FA Cup the club's best effort was the quarter-finals of 1921-2 while in the League, ninth place in 1920-21 was the highest they could manage. Yet some good players were coming to Highbury in this period. In 1922 wing-half Bob John came to the club from the Southern League

Alf Baker, signed from Huddersfield in 1920. He played 311 times in Arsenal's First Division side, leaving the club in 1931.

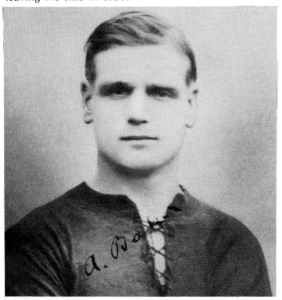

when Arsenal beat off Cardiff for his signature; and in the same year another wing-half, Billy Milne, was signed from Buckie after winning the DCM during the war.

> On 4 February 1922 HRH The Duke Of York (later King George VI) became the first royal visitor to Highbury when he watched the game against Newcastle United. Arsenal first played before a reigning monarch on 4 December 1920 when King George V watched the game between Chelsea and Arsenal at Stamford Bridge.

In 1923 Belfast-born right-back Alex Mackie joined Arsenal from Forth River and another Irishman, Alec Kennedy, signed. The left-back was yet another Toby Mercer recommendation, along with inside-forward Jimmy Hopkins. In 1924-5 goalkeeper Danny Lewis made his Arsenal debut after being transferred from Clapton Orient; Sid Hoar, a left-winger, signed from Luton Town; and centre-forward Jimmy Brain came from Ton Pentre and scored the only goal of his debut match against Spurs.

> During the close season of 1925 Arsenal advertised for a manager in the Athletic News. Part of the advertisement read 'Only people who will not spend big money on transfer fees need apply'. In fact Arsenal had proposed to the 1920 Football League AGM that transfer fees be restricted to £1,650 — a motion that was only narrowly defeated. The successful applicant to the advertisement in 1925 was Herbert Chapman.

In the close season of 1925 Charlie Buchan returned to the club which had lost him over a row concerning eleven shillings in expenses before World War I. Buchan had gone to Leyton before signing for Sunderland. Now he returned at the age of thirty-three on the basis of a £2,000 transfer fee plus £100 for each goal he scored, in his first season with Arsenal—he scored twenty-one and Sunderland collected another £2,100. Goalkeeper Bill Harper also signed for Arsenal in 1925. Harper was one of the first signings made by Herbert Chapman, who had succeeded Leslie Knighton after the Arsenal boss moved on to Bournemouth.

The arrival of Herbert Chapman at Arsenal marked the rebirth of the club—some may say the birth itself of the Arsenal we know today. The period from 1925-34 will always be known as 'the

Chapman era'. He came from Huddersfield, where he had set that famous old Yorkshire club well on the way to a hat-trick of First Division championships. And he was soon to do the same for Arsenal. Chapman was a man ahead of his time. He had pioneered, among other things, floodlit football, the numbering of players, and the white football. Unfortunately for the game, the rulers of football were not quite ready for Herbert Chapman.

But Arsenal were. In his first season, when he was also busy pioneering the 'third back' and 'W' formations to counter the changes in the offside law, Chapman steered Arsenal to the quarter-finals of the FA Cup and to runners-up in the First Division — the highest position ever achieved by a London club at that time. Buchan captained the side and Tom Parker, Southampton's England international right-back, together with Joe Hulme, a £3,500 winger from Blackburn Rovers, came during the season, Hulme making fifteen appearances and Parker seven. Hulme also played for England against Wales and for the Football League against the Army.

> Between 3 April 1926 and 26 December 1929
> Arsenal right-back Tom Parker played 154
> consecutive league matches.

It was after a disasterous game at Newcastle on 3 October — when United beat Arsenal 7-0 — that Chapman decided to move centre-half Butler deep into defence and bring Andy Neil to link up in midfield. Two days later Arsenal beat West Ham 4-0 at Upton Park and Chapman's theory was vindicated. From narrowly missing relegation in the previous two seasons, Arsenal climbed to runners-up, five points behind Chapman's former club Huddersfield, while Jimmy Brain broke the Gunners' individual scoring record with thirty-four League goals. In the FA Cup, Arsenal went through to the last eight before losing 2-1 at Swansea.

Chapman had steered Arsenal to runners-up — and it was only the beginning. A year later the Gunners were in the FA Cup Final at Wembley. The run started at Sheffield United in the third round where Hulme, Brain and Buchan gave Arsenal a 3-2 win. At Port Vale in the next round, an own goal by Parker put Vale ahead before Buchan equalised; then poor Parker gave away a penalty and it was the eighty-eighth minute before Brain earned Arsenal a replay, which they won 1-0, thanks to Buchan's goal. Brain and Buchan were on target in the 2-0 home win over Liverpool in the fifth round and in the quarter-finals it was the turn of Butler and Blyth to earn

Arsenal a 2-1 home win over Wolves. Arsenal were now in their first FA Cup semi-final since 1906-7 and when they met Southampton at Stamford Bridge, Hulme and Buchan eased them into their first FA Cup Final against Cardiff City.

It was Cardiff's second Final in three years — they had lost the 1925 game to Sheffield United — although only four of that side, Farquharson, Nelson, Hardy and Keenor had survived to fight again against Arsenal. Cardiff were at their heights. In 1923-4 they were only pipped to the First Division title on goal average. How fickle are the fortunes of football, though, because in 1934 they were applying for re-election to the Third Division South! But on Cup Final day 1927, the whole world belonged to the Bluebirds from Ninian Park. The game see-sawed either way, with Buchan shining for Arsenal and Curtis for Cardiff. After seventy-five minutes there was no score and it appeared that the game would be the first Wembley Final to go into extra-time.

Arsenal 1927, including the eleven players who played in Arsenal's first-ever FA Cup final. Back row, left to right: Cope, Baker, Parker, Lewis, Butler, John, Kennedy, Seddon. Front row: Tom Whittaker, Hulme, Buchan, Brain, Blyth, Hoar, Herbert Chapman.

Then disaster struck Arsenal, Hugh Ferguson, the Cardiff centre-forward, collected a throw-in and swung over a low cross-shot which Arsenal goalkeeper Danny Lewis appeared to have well covered. But Cardiff's Davies and Irving were powering in on the Gunners' goalkeeper. The Welsh international clawed at the ball and it somehow skidded off his body, evaded his grasping fingers, and rolled gently into the Arsenal net. Cardiff became the first — and, so far, only — side to take the FA Cup out of England. In the dressing room Lewis admitted that he had hurled away his loser's medal on the way from the pitch. Some Arsenal players found it for him — but his action was a measure of the intense disapointment he and the other Gunners felt that day.

Arsenal finished eleventh in the First Division and during the season Herbert Roberts, a red-haired centre-half from Oswestry Town, made his

Lewis's fatal slip. The ball somehow eludes the Arsenal goalkeeper in the 1927 FA Cup final and the trophy goes to Cardiff City — and out of England for the only time.

Charlie Buchan dives for a cross but Cardiff goalkeeper Farquharson punches the ball away during the historic 1927 final.

debut. He was soon to take over from Butler to become one of the most famous pivots in the history of the game. Two other players who made their Arsenal debuts in 1926-7 were Jack Lambert, Doncaster Rovers inside-forward, who played his first game in partnership with Joe Hulme at Bolton on 6 September; and Notts County's left-back, Horace Cope, who came to Highbury in December and made eleven appearances in the League.

Season 1927-8 was a high scoring time for Arsenal—at both ends of the pitch. They scored eighty-two and conceded eighty-six in finishing tenth. The pattern was set in the first few games when Arsenal lost the opening match at Bury 5-1 and then beat Burnley 4-1 and Sheffield United 6-1 in their first two home games. The return match at Bramall Lane saw United storm into a 4-0 lead after just seventeen minutes before Arsenal came back to 4-3 by half-time, eventually losing 6-4. When the last game of the season came round, Everton's centre-forward, Dixie Dean, needed a hat-trick against Arsenal at Goodison Park to beat George Camsell's 1926-7 League record of fifty-nine goals in a season. On 5 May 1928, Dean got his hat-trick and broke the record, but Arsenal still managed a point in the 3-3 draw. In the FA Cup Arsenal reached their second successive semi-final before losing 1-0 to Blackburn Rovers at Leicester. And during the season a young left-back from Kettering called Eddie Hapgood made three appearances in an Arsenal first team shirt. Another piece of Chapman's jigsaw was slotting into place.

1928 saw two significant moves at Highbury. Charles Buchan retired, bringing to an end his illustrious career; and Arsenal signed a replacement in David Jack, the man who scored the first goal in the first Wembley FA Cup Final. The Jack signing shocked all football because he seemed settled in Lancashire. But Herbert Chapman and Bob Wall—who had been on the administrative staff at Highbury since February 1928—met the Bolton chairman and manager and Jack became an Arsenal player for a then record fee of £10,890.

The signing of David Jack for the first five-figure transfer fee in October 1928 was the end of days of negotiating, during which time Chapman and George Allison had beaten down Bolton's original asking price of £13,000. In the end Chapman got his man; and sixteen-year-old Bob Wall, himself to become a great name at Arsenal, saw at first hand how the old maestro operated. Jack made his Arsenal debut on 27 October 1928 against Liverpool at Highbury and helped the Gunners to a 4-4 draw after South African Gordon Hodgson's hat-trick for the Merseysiders had

left Arsenal trailing 3-1. Despite an injury to Roberts, the Gunners grabbed a point. Arsenal finished ninth and in the FA Cup, that unlucky man, Tom Parker, put through his own net to give Aston Villa a 1-0 quarter-final win at Villa Park.

In 1930 Arsenal won the FA Cup for the first time, and in doing so, unleashed on football the most dynamic left-wing partnership, possibly of all time, Alex James and Cliff Bastin. Bastin was the 'Boy Wonder' signed from Exeter City for £2,000 in 1929 at the age of seventeen. He looked so young that the doorman at Highbury once refused to admit him; a few weeks later the fast, direct winger was playing at Wembley. Alex James, of the famous baggy shorts, also came to Highbury in 1929. The Scottish international inside-left—one of the 'Blue Devils' who won 5-1 at Wembley in 1928—cost Arsenal £9,000 from Preston North End. He was worth every penny.

Arsenal Football club reached the 1930s on the threshold of greatness. Perhaps the exact moment when the team reached that magical mixture, when the Chapman cocktail finally blended ready for the great days ahead, can be marked down to a day in April 1930 when, at the end of a long season, Sheffield United visited Highbury for a First Division game. Arsenal were going to finish fourteenth and United would miss relegation by the skin of their teeth. To everyone's surprise, Sheffield opened the scoring. Then a ball was played fast out of Arsenal's defence and wee James made as if to intercept it. Instead, he lifted his foot over the ball and let it go to where Lambert was ready to take it through a mesmerised United defence for the equaliser. That was the moment when Arsenal's success story began. They tore Sheffield United to shreds. The Blades of Yorkshire were themselves cut to pieces. Arsenal won 8-1.

Nine days later, on the Monday before the FA Cup Final, Arsenal took part in a most amazing match at Leicester. They came back from 3-1 down to draw level and then each team scored in turn until they had completed a unique 6-6 draw. Dave Halliday, signed from Sunderland, scored four, and Cliff Bastin nabbed two. Halliday, a player who scored 164 goals for Sunderland and who was the Wearsiders' record marksman in 1928-9, did not play in the 1930 FA Cup Final for Arsenal.

In fact, the prolific goalscorer's four goals against Leicester were exactly half the total he scored for Arsenal. After fifteen games and eight goals he was off to Manchester City.

Arsenal's FA Cup run in 1930 began with a 2-0 home win over Chelsea (Lambert and Bastin), and then involved two ties with Birmingham before Alf Baker got the winner from the penalty spot at St Andrew's. Lambert and Bastin saw Arsenal through 2-0 at Middlesbrough and in the quarter-final against West Ham at Upton Park, Lambert (2) and Baker made it 3-0 for the Gunners and put them into the semi-final against Hull City, a side already destined to be relegated to the Third Division North that season. On paper there could not have been an easier tie. Yet how wrong were the pundits' forecasts! After thirty minutes of the game at Leeds, Hull led 2-0, thanks to an error by Lewis — who seemed jinxed in Cup-ties — and an own goal by Eddie Hapgood.

In the second-half David Jack reduced Hull's lead and eight minutes from time Cliff Bastin equalised with a stinging left-foot shot and the Tigers were left to dwell on what might have been. In the second game at Villa Park, Hull had a player sent off and David Jack was again on target as Arsenal moved into their second FA Cup Final with a 1-0 win. Their opponents in the 1930 game at Wembley were Herbert Chapman's old club, Huddersfield Town. Poor Dan Lewis missed the game. Trying out a knee injury in that amazing 6-6 draw at Leicester he broke down and into his place stepped Londoner Charlie Preedy, who had signed from Wigan that season.

Most people remember the 1930 Final for the fact that the German airship Graf Zeppelin roared over the stadium during the game. But for Arsenal fans the real thrills were on the pitch. In the first quarter-of-an-hour, Bastin, Lambert and Jack all came near to opening the scoring for Arsenal while Jackson went close for Huddersfield. Then

Preedy stops a Huddersfield attack in the 1930 FA Cup final.

Arsenal scored a controversial goal. James was fouled by Goodall and before the Town defence had time to organise itself, the little Scotsman had played the free-kick to Bastin and the left-winger gave him a return pass which James rocketed home. The Huddersfield players were furious, maintaining that the referee Mr Tom Crew had not blown for the kick to be taken. Crew confirmed that he had waved James to take it and the goal stood. In the second-half a left-wing move by John, James and Bastin ended with Jack Lambert streaking between the Huddersfield full-backs to make it 2-0. For the first time, the FA Cup was destined for the Highbury boardroom.

A great day for the Gunners! Tom Parker receives the FA Cup from King George V after Arsenal had beaten Huddersfield 2-0 at Wembley.

The game signalled the start of an amazing run for Arsenal. In ten seasons they won the FA Cup twice, the First Division title five times, reached the FA Cup Final as losers once, and finished runners-up in the League the same season. Never before or since has a First Division club enjoyed so much success in such a short space of time. Arsenal were most certainly the Team of the Decade. The 1930s may have been a time of depression for many. For Arsenal fans they were only good times.

The season after their first FA Cup Final win Arsenal took the First Division title for the first time. And how they did it! The 1930-1 season is remembered for the records broken by Arsenal on their way to the championship. They gained sixty-six points—three more than the previous best by Huddersfield in 1925; twenty-eight wins equalled West Brom's 1920 record; and four defeats was the lowest since Preston went undefeated in the League's first season in 1888-9. Arsenal also beat the old goalscoring record with 127 goals, although Villa—with 128—also surpassed that figure to hold the new record. And Jack Lambert

scored thirty-eight League goals to beat Brain's 1925-6 individual record.

Arsenal's first First Division title win came in this fashion:

1930-31

	P	W	D	L	F	A	Pts
Arsenal	*42*	*28*	*10*	*4*	*127*	*59*	*66*
Aston Villa	*42*	*25*	*9*	*8*	*128*	*78*	*59*
Sheffield Wed.	*42*	*22*	*8*	*12*	*102*	*72*	*52*

Arsenal's league scorers were: Lambert 38, Jack 31, Bastin 28, Hulme 14, James 5, Brain 4, John 2, Williams 2, Johnstone 1, Jones 1, Roberts 1.

Arsenal took the FA Cup to Blackpool for the opening day of the League season on 30 August 1930 and won 4-1 in a game in which the eccentric Dutch goalkeeper Gerry Keyser made his debut. Keyser was one of three goalkeepers used by Arsenal in that first championship season. The Dutchman played twelve games, Charlie Preedy eleven, and Bill Harper nineteen. Only one member of the FA Cup Final side did not make a major contribution to the First Division title. Alf Baker was troubled with injury all season and made just one appearance—against Huddersfield on 7 March—which turned out to be his last. Baker had started games in every one of the ten outfield positions for Arsenal and played in goal when Lewis was carried off at Villa Park to achieve his ambition of playing in every possible position for the Gunners.

When Arsenal entertained Blackpool in the return fixture on 27 December 1930, a young defender called George Male—signed from Clapham the previous May—made his debut. It was the first of 285 League appearances. Arsenal won that match 7-1 with hat-tricks from Brain and Jack. Male—who had toured Holland with Arsenal as an amateur—had an early taste of the success he would experience at Highbury. The Gunners stormed to their first title. They won the first six matches, scoring twenty-two goals in the process, and in two matches early in 1931 they hit fifteen goals, beating Grimsby 9-1 and Derby 6-3. The previous November, Chelsea led Arsenal 1-0 with thirty minutes to play in the game at Stamford Bridge when Jack grabbed a hat-trick and the Gunners romped home 5-1. Chelsea surprisingly knocked Arsenal out of the fourth round of the FA Cup but the Gunners stayed on target for the League and when they won 1-0 at Grimsby on 11 April they had set up a new points record.

Arsenal were now in the winning habit and although 1931-2 saw them lose their League title to Everton—seven points from the last four matches was not good enough after Arsenal had lost two games to Sheffield United over Christmas—they went back to Wembley for another FA Cup Final, where probably the most controversial goal ever scored in a Cup Final helped rob them of the trophy. Arsenal's Cup run began with the easiest of ties, a home game against Darwen of the Lancashire Combination. New goalkeeper Frank Moss, who was signed from Oldham Athletic in 1931, watched as Arsenal ran up eleven goals (Bastin 4, Jack 3, Lambert 2 and Hulme 2).

Former Arsenal goalkeeper Bill Harper could not stop the Gunners beating Plymouth 4-2 in the fourth round, and a brilliant display disposed of Portsmouth at Fratton Park in the fifth. Herbert Roberts moved up to score the only goal of the quarter-final at Huddersfield and Cliff Bastin's last-minute goal decided the semi-final against Manchester City at Villa Park. Meanwhile, Newcastle United had beaten Chelsea 2-1 at Huddersfield and the country was all set for a Gunners v Magpies FA Cup Final.

In the week before the Final there were doubts about the fitness of Hulme and James and after a controversial newspaper article—which 'announced' the team before James and Hulme had got as far as their fitness tests—Herbert Chapman called the two players from Highbury, where they were receiving treatment, to Arsenal's training camp at Brighton. Both men underwent rigorous tests and were pronounced fit. Then a press cameraman asked James for 'just one more picture' and as Tom Whittaker, the Arsenal trainer, and James closed for a tackle, the wee Scotsman's knee 'went' again. Chapman named his team with Cliff Bastin moving inside to take James's shirt while Welsh international left-half, Bob John, moved to outside-left with the unknown George Male making his Cup-tie debut as a left-half at Wembley.

Arsenal were expected to win and after fifteen minutes they took the lead when Newcastle's goalkeeper McInroy and right-back Nelson misjudged Hulme's cross and John, closing from the wing, had the easiest task to push the ball home. Arsenal might have scored again when McInroy dropped a long shot from the Gunner's Welsh international right-half, Charlie Jones, and Nelson scrambled the ball clear. United's left-winger Tommy Lang was giving Parker a lot of trouble and several times only timely tackles by Hapgood and Roberts came to the rescue. Seven minutes from half-time came the controversial goal. United centre-half Davey Davidson intercepted

Hapgood's intended pass to Lambert and sent Jimmy Richardson away down the right. Richardson caught up with the ball by the goal-line and with it still bouncing he hooked back a low centre to where Allen was waiting to turn it into the Arsenal net.

David Jack heads towards the Newcastle goal during the 1932 FA Cup final.

The Gunners defence stood waiting for the referee, Mr W. F. Harper, to signal a goal-kick but instead he pointed to the centre-spot. Newcastle were level and Arsenal's protests were in vain. Various photographs and film 'stills' have suggested that the ball *was* out of play, but the camera does lie and what mattered was that the referee thought it was still in play. After twenty-seven minutes of the second-half Newcastle went ahead when Roberts miskicked—his only mistake of a brilliant afternoon—and Allen made it 2-1 to take the Cup to Tyneside.

Arsenal's disappointment was intense and yet—even allowing for the doubtful nature of Newcastle's equaliser—there could have been no complaints about the final destination of the trophy. But Gunners fans could soon put that afternoon at Wembley behind them. For the next three seasons Arsenal never let go of the First Division title. Their hat-trick equalled that of

Herbert Chapman's former club, Huddersfield Town and although a great feat in its own right, was just part of the magnificent record which Arsenal created in the 1930s.

Throughout the summer of 1932 Highbury's new West Stand took shape and the gound was unrecognisable from the one to which the club had moved twenty years earlier. Early fans had used muddy banks of earth excavated from the Piccadilly Line to give them a better perch. Now they

> Herbert Chapman spent weeks negotiating with London Transport to change the name of Gillespie Road Underground Station. From 5 November 1932 it became known as Arsenal. In the same year Highbury Stadium became officially restyled Arsenal Stadium.

had a stadium to match their great club. The 1932-3 season reached the half-way stage with Arsenal having dropped only six points in a run which saw them beat Leicester 8-2, Sheffield United 9-2, Wolves 7-1, and Sunderland 6-1, with Hulme netting a hat-trick. The home match against Derby on 8 October 1932 saw Arsenal leading 3-1 through Coleman (2) and Hulme, before Herbert Roberts put two goals past his own keeper after being deceived by pinpoint centres from Derby's Sammy Crooks. Crooks told me years later: 'It came off once so I decided to do it again!' Roberts said nothing but afterwards, Alex James remarked, 'He didn't half give himself a look!'

In November 1934 England beat Italy 3-2 at Highbury. The side contained seven Gunners players — a record number supplied by one club to the England side. Tom Whittaker completed the day by being trainer to the international team. The Gunners' proud manager George Allison (extreme left) is pictured here with his men: Copping, Bowden, Male, Moss, Drake, Hapgood, Bastin and Whittaker.

Right in the middle of Arsenal's title-winning campaign came one of the most staggering giant killing acts in the history of the FA Cup. On 14 January 1933 Arsenal were drawn away to Third Division North side, Walsall. The pundits did not give the Midlanders a chance. They cost a total of £69 — Arsenal's team was valued at £30,000. But this may have been one occasion when the great Chapman made a mistake. Hapgood was ruled out by injury, while Bob John, Tim Coleman and Jack Lambert had all had flu. In addition Joe Hulme had been out of the side through indifferent form. But instead of bringing back Hulme's experience, or perhaps risking one or two of the flu victims, Chapman chose four reserves. Only one — Norman Sidey — had played in the first team before, and that had been just for one game. The others, left-back Tommy Black from Scottish junior football, and former London amateurs outside-right Billy Warnes and centre-forward Charlie Walsh, had no First Division experience.

But Arsenal still fielded seven internationals and even the fact that Walsh was so nervous that he put on his boots before his stockings did not worry Chapman unduly. But the tight, little Walsall ground and the hard tackling of the Third Division side began to unsettle the Arsenal aristocrats. Walsh missed a 'sitter', and Black became increasingly frustrated. Fifteen minutes into the second-half Walsall went ahead when Gilbert Alsop headed home Lee's corner. Five minutes later, Black committed a stupid foul and Sheppard scored from the spot to give Walsall a sensational 2-0 win. Within a week Black was transferred to Plymouth, inside a month Walsh moved to Brentford, and in May, Warnes was sold to Norwich.

Of the Arsenal newcomers only Sidey remained and he gave loyal service. Although he played only forty games before retiring in 1938, due to being overshadowed by Roberts and Joy, Sidey could always be relied upon to give his best when drafted

into the side. Arsenal soon shook off the effects of that dreadful result and five wins on the trot, including victories over close rivals Villa and Sheffield Wednesday, gave them the title with two games still to play. One player to establish a regular place in the side was Ray Bowden, signed from Plymouth early in 1933. Bowden filled all three inside-forward positions as Arsenal stormed through the 1930s.

In 1933-4 Arsenal lifted the title again, but the season was marred by the death of the great Herbert Chapman. Chapman died, as he had lived, for football. Tom Whittaker knew he had a cold and tried to talk him out of going to Guildford to see a player. Chapman refused, sat out the match in freezing weather, and three days later, on 6 January 1934, he was dead. That afternoon Arsenal played Sheffield Wednesday at a strangely subdued Highbury and drew 1-1. The players were affected greatly by the shock of their old mentor's death but they got back to form the following Saturday — having attended Chapman's funeral in midweek — and beat Luton Town 1-0 in the third round of the FA Cup.

Chapman's death was a tragedy, more so since he did not live to see Arsenal's great hat-trick of championships. Four months before he died Chapman made his last big signing for the Gunners when he brought Sheffield United's Irish-born centre-forward Jimmy Dunne to Highbury. Dunne made his debut against Middlesbrough on 30 September and although he did not score, Arsenal won 6-0 and they were to take the title again. Twice during the season the attendance record was broken at Highbury. On 31 January, Spurs were the visitors in a re-arranged midweek game and 68,828 saw Arsenal lose 3-1 after

Hapgood conceded a penalty, John miskicked and then Male was robbed by Evans. On Good Friday, 30 March, Derby attracted 69,070 who saw Arsenal's 1-0 win put them on top of the table. Although Huddersfield temporarily regained the lead, Arsenal were soon back on top. In March 1934, Southampton's high-scoring Ted Drake signed for Arsenal and played in the last ten games, scoring seven goals. In the FA Cup, Arsenal went out in the quarter-finals to Aston Villa. Arsenal's new manager, facing the impossible task of following Chapman, was the club's director, George Allison, who eventually became secretary-manager.

For Arsenal's third successive championship season of 1934-5, several new faces were in the team. Jack, Lambert, Coleman and Jones had all played their last games for Arsenal the previous season and newcomers included Wilf Copping of Leeds United and Jack Crayston of Bradford, both wing-halves, and forwards Alf Kirchen from Norwich and Bob Davidson from St. Johnstone. Arsenal started April already four points ahead of the rest and six points over Easter — including an 8-0 drubbing of Middlesbrough whose side included ex-Arsenal men Ralph Birkett and Ernie Coleman — sent them away on their own. Ted Drake set up what is still Arsenal's individual League scoring record with forty-two goals in forty-one matches and Arsenal fans could forgive their side being knocked out of the FA Cup quarter-finals by Sheffield Wednesday.

Grimsby defenders can only look on helplessly as Arsenal score another goal in their 6-0 win over the Mariners in September 1935.

From a League point of view, season 1935-6 was a let-down for Arsenal. They finished sixth after their triumphs of the previous three seasons and the only real highlight came at Villa Park on 14 December 1935 when Ted Drake scored a record seven goals as Arsenal trounced Aston Villa 7-1. Drake scored with his first six shots but poor George Allison missed this epic — he was at home in bed with the flu! Eventual champions Sunderland gave Arsenal two fine games, scoring first on the opening day of the season before Drake (2) and Bastin gave the Gunners a 3-1 win; and then winning a thrilling game 5-4 at Roker Park after Arsenal had pulled back from 4-1 down to 4-3 before Sunderland took both points.

Arsenal's hat-trick of First Division Championship wins looked like this:							
1932-33							
	P	*W*	*D*	*L*	*F*	*A*	*Pts*
Arsenal	*42*	*25*	*8*	*9*	*118*	*61*	*58*
Aston Villa	*42*	*23*	*8*	*11*	*92*	*67*	*54*
Sheffield Wed.	*42*	*21*	*9*	*12*	*80*	*68*	*51*
1933-34							
Arsenal	*42*	*25*	*9*	*8*	*75*	*47*	*59*
Huddersfield	*42*	*23*	*10*	*9*	*90*	*61*	*56*
Spurs	*42*	*21*	*7*	*14*	*79*	*56*	*49*
1934-35							
Arsenal	*42*	*23*	*12*	*7*	*115*	*46*	*58*
Sunderland	*42*	*19*	*16*	*7*	*90*	*51*	*54*
Sheffield Wed.	*42*	*18*	*13*	*11*	*70*	*64*	*49*

April 1936 and Arsenal hold aloft the FA Cup yet again.

But if Arsenal missed out on a fourth consecutive First Division title in 1935-6, they went to Wembley and won the FA Cup for the second time. In February that season Arsenal supplied England with six players for the midweek international against Wales — Hapgood, Male, Crayston, Bowden, Drake and Bastin — but Drake was badly injured in the game and was out for ten weeks. Arsenal had an injury crisis for Roberts went down with a muscle strain and then on 8 February — just before the fifth round tie with Newcastle — Frank Moss was injured again at Blackburn and Leslie Compton took over in goal. For the Newcastle tie Arsenal brought back Alex Wilson, a young Scot from Greenock Morton. Sidey was at centre-half in place of Roberts and after a 3-3 draw Roberts returned to help Arsenal win the replay at Highbury 3-0. A quarter-final tie with Barnsley was won 4-1 and then Arsenal met Grimsby at Huddersfield in the semi-final where Cliff Bastin scored the only goal of the game.

Drake was fit for the Wembley game against Second Division Sheffield United and again the unlucky man to step down was Pat Beasley. Beasley had missed the 1932 Final when Joe Hulme was declared fit. Wilson retained his place in the Arsenal goal — Moss was still unfit — and for the first seventy-five minutes of the game Arsenal held the edge without being able to score the vital goal. Then, fifteen minutes from time, James rolled the ball to Bastin who went down the wing and then squared a pass to where Drake was waiting to crash a great left-foot shot past the helpless John Smith. Drake limped through the remaining minutes — but he had done his job and given Arsenal the Cup.

Frank Moss retired — he scored a goal on 16 March 1935 against Everton after playing up front following his original shoulder injury — and in April 1936 Arsenal signed another goalkeeper named George Swindin from Bradford City. Swindin made his debut in the 2-0 defeat at Brentford on 3 September 1936 and played nineteen times between Arsenal's posts. Frank Boulton, from Bath City, played twenty-one times, and Alex Wilson, who took over from Moss for most of the previous season managed only two games.

In 1936-7 — for the first time since 1931-2 — Arsenal won nothing. The First Division was beyond them by the end of October, although they did climb to the top in the New Year and stayed there until 10 April when Manchester City beat them 2-0 at Maine Road to give themselves the title. But Arsenal's poor start had cost them dearly. In the FA Cup they reached the sixth round before West Brom beat them 3-1 in stark contrast to the previous stage when Drake's four

The official club photograph of the 1936 Cup winners. Back row, left to right: Male, Crayston, Wilson, Roberts, Drake, Hapgood. Front row: George Allison, Hulme, Bowden, James, Bastin, Tom Whittaker. Seated: Beasley, Copping.

Jack Crayston, signed by George Allison from Bradford in 1934, he gave the club tremendous service until the outbreak of war. He later became manager of the Gunners.

Arsenal players Eddie Hapgood (left) and Frank Moss take a pre-season training stroll with trainer Tom Whittaker in August 1936.

goals had helped them demolish Burnley 7-1. On 26 September 1936 Denis Compton made his debut on the left-wing in the 2-2 draw with Derby at Highbury and he and his brother Leslie—who had signed in February 1932 and who was in Arsenal's first team before the end of that season—made fourteen and fifteen appearances respectively. Bernard Joy, the famous England amateur international centre-half, made six appearances following his debut in 1935-6.

In 1937-8 Arsenal became champions for the fifth time with the remarkably small points total of fifty-two. Alex James played his last game for Arsenal on 6 June 1937 when he turned out against Feyenoord in Rotterdam. His career with the club had spanned all its great days from 1928-9 in which time he had played 231 games in the League and scored twenty-six goals, captaining the side for five seasons. The race for the title was between Arsenal—without James for the first time in almost a decade—and Wolves, and it was not decided until the last day of the season. Wolves were a point ahead of Arsenal and each side had one game to play. Arsenal beat Bolton 5-0 on 7 May 1938 and on the same day Wolves

A picture which captures the greatness of Alex James, seen here leaving Manchester City's Sam Barkas, Jackie Bray and Matt Busby marooned as he streaks through their defence during a First Division match in the 1930s.

went down 1-0 at Sunderland to give the Gunners another title by the slenderest of margins. Ted Drake (seventeen) and Cliff Bastin (fifteen) led the scorers, with Bastin and Wilf Copping missing only four games each. In the FA Cup Arsenal lost 1-0 in the fifth round at Preston.

Top three of the First Division when Arsenal won yet another title in 1937-38 were:

	P	W	D	L	F	A	Pts
Arsenal	*42*	*21*	*10*	*11*	*77*	*44*	*52*
Wolves	*42*	*20*	*11*	*11*	*72*	*49*	*51*
Preston	*42*	*16*	*17*	*9*	*64*	*44*	*49*

Bob John retired in 1937 after breaking the club record with 421 Football League matches. The present record is held by George Graham with exactly 500 games.

Before the start of the 1938-9 season George Allison broke the transfer record by paying Wolves £14,500 for their international inside-left, Bryn Jones. Although Jones scored on his debut for the Gunners — against Portsmouth — he never justified the big fee. Perhaps the tag of the world's costliest footballer weighed heavily on him. Jones could not fit into the Alex James mould some of the fans unfairly expected him to do and along with Bastin, Crayston and Les Jones, another Welsh international who came from Coventry in 1937, he failed to recapture his form. Younger players came into the side, including another Welsh international, Horace Cumner, and Reg

Lewis, an inside-forward from Nunhead who made his debut against Everton on New Year's Day 1938 and who played fifteen games in 1938-9. Arsenal finished fifth in the First Division in the last full season before the war. In the FA Cup they were knocked out by Chelsea in the third round.

Arsenal played in four FA Cup finals between the wars. The teams and results are:
23 April 1927 (v Cardiff City): D. Lewis, T. Parker, A. Kennedy, A. Baker, J. Butler, R. John, J. Hulme, C. Buchan (capt), J. Brain, W. Blyth, S. Hoar. Lost 0-1.
26 April 1930 (v Huddersfield Town): C. Preedy, T. Parker (capt), E. Hapgood, A. Baker, W. Seddon, R. John, J. Hulme, D. Jack, J. Lambert, A. James, C. Bastin. Won 2-0 (James, Lambert).
23 April 1932 (v Newcastle United): F. Moss, T. Parker (capt), E. Hapgood, C. Jones, H. Roberts, G. Male, J. Hulme, D. Jack, J. Lambert, C. Bastin, R. John. Lost 1-2 (John).
25 April 1936 (v Sheffield United): A. Wilson, G. Male, E. Hapgood, W. Crayston, H. Roberts, W. Copping, J. Hulme, E. Bowden, E. Drake, A. James (capt), C. Bastin. Won 1-0 (Drake).

After just three games of the 1939-40 football season — Wolves (2-2), Blackburn Rovers (1-0) and Sunderland (5-2) — Arsenal's Football League career was suspended until 1946-7. During the war the club played in regional competitions and wrote their name on a few trophies, but the real golden days were over for the moment. Arsenal had risen from a fairly ordinary First Division club to one of the greatest in the world within the space of ten years. Surely no club will ever establish such a reputation in that manner ever again?

Preston's Fairbrother saves from Arsenal's Kirchen during the Football League War Cup final replay at Blackburn in 1941. Arsenal lost 2-1.

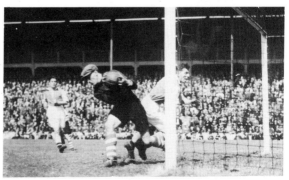

For the first full post-war First Division season Arsenal had the services of several new faces. Full-backs Wally Barnes, from Southampton, and Joe Wade, from amateur soccer, had signed during the war. Bristol youngster Arthur Milton, a skilful right-winger, had also signed in the last days of the war, joining Arsenal as a schoolboy in April 1945 and signing professional forms in July 1946. Jimmy Logie was already on the clubs books when war broke out—he had signed from Scottish junior side Lochore Welfare—and names like Bastin, Joy, Bryn Jones, Lewis, Male, Scott, Nelson and Swindin were all at Highbury in the 1930s. So, too, were the Compton brothers, and they would soon be joined by famous names like Joe Mercer, Ronnie Rooke and a name that was to become famous, Ray Daniel.

Ronnie Rooke, signed from Fulham when Arsenal were desperate for a goalscorer in December 1946 and repaid them with twelve goals in his first ten matches.

Arsenal's—indeed football's—return to some sanity came in the FA Cup of 1945-6 which was played on a two-legged basis. Sadly, Arsenal made no impact on this unique season, losing 6-0 to West Ham at Upton Park in the third round first-leg. Even a goal by Cumner, which gave Arsenal a 1-0 win in the return leg, could do nothing to compensate the Gunners. They were down and very much out.

Birmingham's left-winger Edwards beats George Swindin during a Football League South game in February 1946. The game was played at Tottenham, Arsenal's wartime home.

Remembrance Day 1946 and Arsenal and Racing Club de Paris observe a silence at the Parc des Princes. The annual series of matches started in 1930 and continued until the French club's demise.

Arsenal's team for their first Football League match since World War II (away to Wolves on 31 August 1946) was: Swindin, Scott, Male, Nelson, B. Joy, Curtis, McPherson, Sloan, Lewis, Logie, Bastin. Arsenal lost 6-1. Bryn Jones declined to play as he felt he was not fully fit. Paddy Sloan was dropped after three games in Arsenal's forward line but reverted to right-half in the Football Combination and soon won his place back as a wing-half, playing a further twenty-seven games and being capped for Ireland in his new position. The former Tranmere Rovers man moved to Sheffield United in 1948.

ing out for Ireland at rugby and soccer in successive weeks. In the FA Cup Arsenal and Chelsea had to play their third round tie three times before two goals by Tommy Lawton settled the matter in Chelsea's favour at White Hart Lane.

Thanks to some grim weather the 1946-7 soccer season had been the longest on record. But the summer of 1947 was one of the most glorious and Arsenal's Denis Compton spent it rewriting the cricket record books with Middlesex and England as runs just sizzled off his bat. And Compton had

The season started disasterously for Arsenal. Poor Jimmy Logie could not have picked a worse game for his debut as they slid to a 6-1 defeat at Wolves with Lewis getting the lone Gunners goal. After eighteen games Arsenal had gained only eleven points and only 0.142 of a goal stood between them and bottom club Huddersfield Town. The turning point came when Ronnie Rooke came from Fulham and Joe Mercer was signed from Everton. Both were established and experienced players, both at the crossroads of their careers. On his debut against Charlton at Highbury on 14 December 1946, Rooke scored the winning goal to begin a run of twenty-one goals in twenty-four games. Arsenal, with Swindin in tremendous form in goal, and Scott and Barnes at full-back, settled down. They finished the season in thirteenth spot — bad by Arsenal standards but it could have been much worse — and only the left-wing spot caused real problems where no fewer than eleven different players were tried, including the famous Dr Kevin O'Flanagan, who made history by turn-

Tom Whittaker MBE was appointed Arsenal manager in succession to George Allison, who retired in the close season of 1947, and steered Arsenal straight to the title.
Whittaker was born in Aldershot but brought up in Newcastle-upon-Tyne. He joined Arsenal in 1919 as a centre-forward but made the league side as a wing-half and full-back. Whittaker made 64 appearances up to the end of 1924-25 when he was chosen for the FA touring side to Australia where a knee injury ended his career, save for one match in 1929 when as trainer to the FA South African touring side, he played one emergency game — and scored!
Whittaker became Arsenal assistant trainer in 1926 and trainer in 1927. He trained the England side and various FA touring sides and after war service in the RAF — when he was awarded the MBE — he became Arsenal assistant manager at the end of the war.

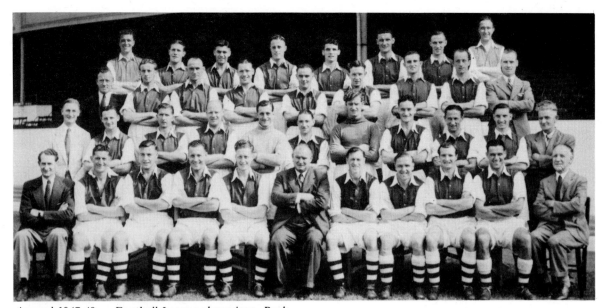

Arsenal 1947-48 — Football League champions. Back row, left to right: L. Compton, D. Clelland, T. Vallance, J. Edington, J. Wade, A. Fields, L. Smith, D. Compton. Second row: D. Cripps (dressing room attendant), N. Smith, E. Collett, J. Sherratt, B. Jones, N. Bowden, A. Horsfield, S. Jones, H. Owen (assistant trainer). Third row: W. R. Wall (assistant secretary), L. Delaney, A. Morgan, G. Male, G. Swindin, J. Logie, E. Platt, J. Sloan, D. Farquhar, E. Holland, W. Milne (trainer). Front row: J. Crayston (assistant manager), R. Rooke, R. Lewis. D. Roper, A. Macauley, T. Whittaker MBE (secretary-manager), J. Mercer, L. Scott, W. Barnes, I. McPherson, J. Shaw (chief representative).

reason to celebrate the 1947-8 soccer season too. Fourteen games in the Gunners shirt qualified him for a First Division Championship medal. Yes, Arsenal took the title to equal Villa's and Sunderland's record of six wins.

The highest attendance ever recorded for a league match was on 17 January 1948 when Arsenal's visit to Maine Road to play Manchester United attracted 83,260 (Old Trafford was still out of use due to wartime bombing).

The previous record also involved Arsenal when 82,905 saw the Gunners play Chelsea at Stamford Bridge on 12 October 1935.

Arsenal started with a 3-1 home win over Sunderland and finished with an 8-0 home thrashing of Grimsby Town. They headed the table from start to finish and conceded only thirty-two goals — a League record. In calling on only eighteen players to win the title they equalled West

Brom's 1919-20 record. And the club enjoyed its best-ever start — their first defeat did not come until 29 November when Derby won 1-0 at Highbury, by which time Arsenal already had twelve wins and five draws in seventeen games. When Ronnie Rooke cracked home four against Grimsby on the last day of the season the title was already secure. Only Bradford's Elliott who scored the goal which gave the Second Division side a shock 1-0 FA Cup third round win over Arsenal, spoiled the Gunners season. Ronnie Rooke and George Swindin played in all games and Don Roper, signed from Southampton in August 1947, Archie Macauley, who came to Arsenal via Rangers, West Ham and Brentford, and Joe Mercer missed only two each. Logie and Scott were absent only three times each, Leslie Compton played thirty-five times, and Ian McPherson twenty-nine. Lewis made twenty-eight appearances.

Arsenal won the 1947-48 First Division title like this:

	P	W	D	L	F	A	Pts
Arsenal	42	23	13	6	81	32	59
Manchester Utd.	42	19	14	9	81	48	52
Burnley	42	20	12	10	56	43	52

Arsenal equalled a record by using only eighteen players to lift the trophy. Leslie Smith played in the last match against Grimsby on 1 May 1948 to bring the total to nineteen but the Championship had been won after the draw at Huddersfield on 10 April. Ronnie Rooke was leading scorer with thirty-three goals.

In 1948-9 Arsenal were dogged by injuries to key players and when Scott was injured playing for England, Barnes had to move to right-back and Lionel Smith switched from centre-half to left-back. Arsenal climbed from fifteenth place in September to fifth spot by Christmas. On 19 February two goals from Lewis helped Arsenal to a 3-1 win over Wolves at Molineux to put an end to Wolves run of nine home wins. Logie scored Arsenal's third and Jesse Pye nailed Wolves goal from the penalty spot after Leslie Compton handled. Arsenal finished the season in fifth place — a good effort after all their injury troubles — and in the FA Cup they beat Spurs 3-0 at Highbury, only to lose 1-0 at Derby's Baseball Ground in the next round. George Male had played his last game for Arsenal at the end of the previous season in that 8-0 trouncing of Grimsby (remember Arsenal beat Blackpool 7-1 on Male's debut in December 1930, so Male ended as he began) and yet more young faces appeared in Arsenal colours for the first time including Ray Daniel who played in the last match of the season. Walsall's Doug Lishman, signed by Arsenal in May 1948, made his debut in 1948-9, scoring twelve goals in twenty-three games; and Alec Forbes, who had scored on his debut in the 1947-8 championship season, also played in over half the games. Peter Goring and Cliff Holton were other young players on the books. In the close season Rooke went to Crystal Palace as player-manager.

In 1949-50 Arsenal won the FA Cup for the third time in five Finals. The Gunners opened the season with four defeats in five games but the introduction of young Peter Goring — twenty-one goals in twenty-nine games — and Freddie Cox, who came from Spurs for a five-figure fee in September 1949 and who was the architect of many of Goring's goals, gave Arsenal new impetus and they finished sixth. Arthur Shaw, a wing-half signed from Brentford, also made his League debut for Arsenal in 1949-50.

Liverpool's Laurie Hughes and Arsenal's Denis Compton tussle during the 1950 FA Cup final.

In the FA Cup Arsenal beat Sheffield Wednesday, Swansea Town, Burnley and Leeds before facing Chelsea in the semi-final at White Hart Lane. Bentley put Chelsea 2-0 up before Cox scored direct from a corner. Then Leslie Compton defied Mercer's orders to stay back and ran forward to head his brother's corner home for the equaliser. In the replay, also at Spurs ground, the score was 0-0 after ninety minutes. In extra-time Cox went off on a solo run and ended it with a great shot to put Arsenal through to Wembley to meet Liverpool.

The 1950 FA Cup Final is best remembered for two brilliant goals by Reg Lewis. The first came after seventeen minutes when Logie took Barnes's pass, and with Goring taking Laurie Hughes out of the middle, the Scot slipped the ball into space where Lewis collected it and stroked a fine low shot past Sidlow. After eighteen minutes of the

Ted Platt misses a cross from West Brom's Williams and Walshe (right of picture) moves in to score. But Arsenal won this midweek First Division game 4-1 in September 1949.

second-half Cox back-heeled inside Spicer and there was Lewis again, streaking through to crack an eighteen-yarder past the Liverpool goalkeeper to bring the FA Cup to Highbury once more.

By the middle of December 1950, Arsenal were riding high in the First Division. Doug Lishman had netted seventeen goals, including four in the 5-1 win over Sunderland, and a hat-trick in the 5-1 win over Fulham. On Christmas Day 1950 Stoke City came to Highbury and won 3-0. Lishman was carried off with a broken leg and George Swindin was also injured that day. It was the turning point of the season for Arsenal. Lewis came back into the side but although he scored eight goals in four-teen games, he could not find Lishman's touch. Jack Kelsey, the young goalkeeper signed from a Welsh junior club in September 1949, made his debut on 24 February 1951 but was unfortunate enough to come up against Charlton's in-form Swedish international centre-forward, Hans Jepp-son, who scored a hat-trick as Charlton won 5-2 at Highbury. Kelsey made four appearances that season and Ted Platt, who had been understudy goalkeeper at Arsenal since 1938, had the rare chance to play as many as seventeen matches.

Arthur Milton made his debut after six years in the wings when he played against Aston Villa on 10 March 1951, and other players to get their first games in an Arsenal first team shirt in 1950-1 were Dave Bowen (seven games), Cliff Holton (ten) and Ben Marden (eleven). Daniel was capped for Wales while still an Arsenal reserve.

One of the great talking points of the season, in addition to Daniel's selection, was the winning of two England caps by thirty-eight-year-old Leslie

Arsenal have the Cup for the third time, equalling Bolton's record of three Wembley wins with their 2-0 win over Liverpool in 1950. Mercer is chaired with the Cup but Reg Lewis (farthest left), scorer of both goals, looks particularly thoughtful.

Compton. The centre-half, in his penultimate season, played against Wales at Sunderland (op-posing Daniel incidentally) to become England's oldest-ever debutant. He played once more against Yugoslavia. The honours were long overdue. Arsenal finished the season in fifth place, the in-juries to Goring and Swindin having enough effect on the team to stunt its early rise. In the FA Cup Arsenal got through to the fifth round before Manchester United beat them with a solitary goal at Old Trafford.

Peter Goring lobs a beautiful ball over the head of Huddersfield goalkeeper Mills to score the Gunners' last goal in their 6-2 First Division win over the Yorkshiremen in September 1950.

1951-2

Arsenal came within an ace of winning the 'Double' of First Division title *and* the FA Cup some twenty years before they finally achieved it. In 1951-2 the Gunners came so close to both trophies, only to miss out on both just as they had done in 1931-2. And, as in 1932, it was Newcastle United who killed off Arsenal's hopes in the second leg of the 'Double', the FA Cup.

Early in August 1951, Tom Whittaker, concerned by Arsenal's advance ticket sales which he knew compared unfavourably with those of neighbouring Spurs who had just won the First Division title, decided that the Gunners needed a box office draw. Soon, he and Joe Shaw were speeding towards Blackpool, then at the height of the holiday season. But Whittaker and Shaw were not going north for the sun — they were hoping to bring back Stanley Matthews. Blackpool's manager, Joe Smith, could not be budged, and even a second visit, when Whittaker threw down his cheque book and told the Blackpool boss to write his own price for the wizard, failed to do the trick, although Matthews admitted: 'Every actor wants to play in the West End — and I would like to play for Arsenal.' The Seasiders would not budge.

If Whittaker failed to find his box office draw, he did find a right-winger to solve his immediate problems. And the man was at Arsenal all the time. Fair-haired Arthur Milton played so well that he found himself in the England side after only twelve games. Then tragedy struck and injury laid him low and he failed to recover his form, giving the eventual number seven spot in the Cup Final team to Freddie Cox.

> *Laurie Scott played his last game for Arsenal in 1951-52 to bring to an end a career spanning 115 league matches. Scott signed for Arsenal from Bradford City in 1937 but had to wait until 1946 for his debut. Although troubled by injury and illness for part of his career, Scott developed into one of the fastest and most stylish backs in the country, playing in seventeen successive internationals for England. He left Arsenal for the player-manager's job at Crystal Palace in October 1951.*

Arsenal were always 'there or thereabouts' as they say in football. In November and December they topped the First Division thanks to hat-tricks in successive home games (v Fulham, WBA and Bolton) by Doug Lishman, who scored four hat-tricks altogether that season and finished top scorer. Until ten days before the Cup Final

Newcastle's Ronnie Simpson foils an Arsenal raid at Wembley. Cliff Holton waits for a slip.

Arsenal were in contention for the title, despite some appalling luck with injuries. Apart from Milton, Daniel, who broke his wrist at Blackpool on Good Friday, Leslie Compton (making his last League appearance for Arsenal), Logie, Shaw, Smith, Lishman, Cox, Forbes and Lewis were all injured during the second-half of the season. With eight games to play in the last fifteen days of the season Arsenal's task was huge. Even the successful conversion of Cliff Holton from full-back to centre-forward—where he scored seventeen goals—could not give Arsenal the necessary lift. And yet only three games stood between the Gunners and that 'Double'—two away League games at Old Trafford and the Hawthorns, and the FA Cup Final. By the time they took the field for the Final Arsenal had lost 6-1 to United and 3-1 to West Brom. Half the dream was already shattered.

If Arsenal had suffered injuries in the League, then fate played its cruellest hand when the 1952 FA Cup Final was only eighteen minutes old. Wally Barnes and United's 'Wor' Jackie Milburn clashed and Barnes went down as though he had been shot. The Welsh international went off, with Don Roper at right-back, and although he came back on briefly, he retired for good, after thirty-four minutes.

Before Barnes's injury, Arsenal—with Ray Daniel playing with a plastic shield over his injured wrist—looked favourites and Swindin had hardly been troubled, while Arsenal had gone close three times. And even when down to ten men the Gunners held their own. With eleven minutes to play there was no score and Arsenal had turned this into one of the most exciting Finals ever staged. The Gunners defence was tight—and they could still make chances up front. Then Arsenal forced a corner. Cox took it and Lishman rose to head it against the Newcastle bar and out for a goal-kick.

It was not to be Arsenal's day. Six minutes from the end United scored. Mitchell rounded Roper and found George Robledo's head. The Chilean nodded the ball against Swindin's post and watched it roll agonisingly over the line. Newcastle's Stanley Seymour summed it up: 'To us the Cup—to Arsenal the Glory.'

First Division results 1951-2

	H	A
Aston Villa	2-1	0-1
Blackpool	4-1	0-0
Bolton	4-2	1-2
Burnley	1-0	1-0
Charlton	2-1	3-1
Chelsea	2-1	3-1
Derby	3-1	2-1
Fulham	4-3	0-0
Huddersfield	2-2	3-2
Liverpool	0-0	0-0
Manchester City	2-2	2-0
Manchester United	1-3	1-6
Middlesbrough	3-1	3-0
Newcastle	1-1	0-2
Portsmouth	4-1	1-1
Preston	3-3	0-2
Stoke	4-1	1-2
Sunderland	3-0	1-4
Tottenham	1-1	2-1
West Brom	6-3	1-3
Wolves	2-2	1-2

Final League Record

P	W	D	L	F	A	Pts	Pos
42	21	11	10	80	61	53	3rd

FA Cup

Rnd 3	Norwich City	(a)	5-0
Rnd 4	Barnsley	(h)	4-0
Rnd 5	Leyton Orient	(a)	3-0
Rnd 6	Luton Town	(a)	3-2
S Final	Chelsea	(n)	1-1
Replay	Chelsea	(n)	3-0
Final	Newcastle	(W)	0-1

n = neutral venue
W = Wembley

Freddie Cox (not in picture) scores Arsenal's second goal in their 3-0 FA Cup semi-final replay win over Chelsea at White Hart Lane.

1952-3

Arsenal won the First Division title for the seventh time, thus eclipsing the records of Sunderland and Aston Villa. But what a tussle it was! For a time Arsenal looked to have lost their chance of breaking the record and it was only on the last day of the season that the issue was settled in the Gunners' favour. In addition the season had its undercurrents when Ray Daniel asked for a transfer after Whittaker had spoken his mind about the centre-half's decision to ignore his manager's instructions in one game. Happily, Daniel stayed until the end of the season and when he did go—to Sunderland—Arsenal had a ready-made replacement in Fulham centre-half Bill Dodgin—son of the Fulham boss of the same name—who left Craven Cottage for Highbury in December 1952.

Wally Barnes missed the entire season after his Cup Final injury of the previous season and when Arsenal kicked off the season at Villa Park, Lewis, Logie, Cox and right-back John Chenhall, who had made his debut the previous season, were all injured. In addition Arthur Milton was playing cricket for Gloucestershire and Whittaker moved Alex Forbes to outside-right and brought young Don Oakes into the side. Oakes repaid Whittaker's faith. He scored the winning goal at Villa Park and then laid on Peter Goring's winner against Manchester United five days later.

Two transfers that did not materialise were Arsenal's bid for Norwich goalkeeper, Ken Nethercott, and Pompey's attempt to sign Cliff Holton. Nethercott's decision not to leave the Canaries left open the door for Jack Kelsey, who had been waiting in the wings, to establish himself in the senior side. Kelsey grabbed the opportunity with both hands and started what was to be an illustrious run. He played twenty-five times, with Swindin making fourteen appearances in his penultimate playing season at Arsenal. And Ted Platts, a perpetual understudy at Highbury since 1938, managed two games. Another defender to establish himself in 1952-3 was Joe Wade. Right-back Wade made his debut in 1946 but not until Barnes was injured did he have the chance of a regular place. He played forty times in Arsenal's title-winning side and was chosen to play for the League.

Arsenal's title challenge was interrupted by the FA Cup and a thrilling sixth round tie at home to Blackpool when Logie's goal meant that the Gunners were level at 1-1 before the tragic accident to Blackpool's Allan Brown. Brown and Kelsey reached the ball at the same time and although the Blackpool player managed to slide the ball past the Welshman, the players collided and Brown's left leg was broken. Never was there a more dramatic nor tragic winner in the quarter-finals of the Cup. Blackpool went to Wembley but Brown missed the great day.

A week after the Blackpool tie Cardiff surprisingly won 1-0 at Arsenal and this seemed to have put the Gunners out of the race for the title. But on 19 March Joe Mercer was injured and moved up to centre-forward in the home game against Preston—who were also on target for the championship—and scored a late equaliser. Arsenal drew 1-1 at Stamford Bridge; then beat Chelsea 2-0 at Highbury over Easter when the Gunners

Joe Mercer, in unfamiliar stripes, gets in a shot as he is challenged by Blackpool's Hugh Kelly. But it was Blackpool who proved the hotshots by beating Arsenal 2-1 in the FA Cup sixth round tie at Highbury in February 1953.

collected five points. Suddenly there was everything to play for and the matter could have been settled at Deepdale on 25 April. But Preston beat Arsenal 2-0 that day and with one match to play the sides were level on fifty-two points.

Preston played their last match at Derby on 29 April where Tom Finney's penalty gave them the win they wanted. Arsenal now had to beat Burnley at Highbury two days later. On 1 May, 51,586 packed the Arsenal ground in torrential rain. On a sea of mud Burnley went ahead after eight minutes but Forbes, Lishman and Logie made it 3-1 before the game was twenty minutes old. Sixteen minutes from the end that was how the score stood. Then Burnley netted again. Finally the whistle blew and the agony was over. Arsenal were champions by one-tenth of a goal.

Arsenal 1952-53. Back row, left to right: Tom Whittaker MBE (manager), R. Marden, J. Wade, P. Goring, D. Bowen, G. Swindin, A. Shaw, T. Chenhall, D. Lishman, F. Cox, W. Milne (trainer). Front row: C. Holton, R. Lewis, R. Daniel, A. Forbes, J. Mercer, W. Barnes, L. Smith, D. Roper. On ground: J. Robertson, J. Logie.

First Division results 1952-3

	H	A
Aston Villa	3-1	2-1
Blackpool	3-1	2-3
Bolton	4-1	6-4
Burnley	3-2	1-1
Cardiff	0-1	0-0
Charlton	3-4	2-2
Chelsea	2-0	1-1
Derby	6-2	0-2
Liverpool	5-3	5-1
Manchester City	3-1	4-2
Manchester United	2-1	0-0
Middlesbrough	2-1	0-2
Newcastle	3-0	2-2
Portsmouth	3-1	2-2
Preston	1-1	0-2
Sheffield Wednesday	2-2	4-1
Stoke	3-1	1-1
Sunderland	1-2	1-3
Tottenham	4-0	3-1
West Brom	2-2	0-2
Wolves	5-3	1-1

Final League Record

P	W	D	L	F	A	Pts	Pos
42	21	12	9	97	64	54	1st

FA Cup

Rnd 3	Doncaster	(h)	4-0
Rnd 4	Bury	(h)	6-2
Rnd 5	Burnley	(a)	2-0
Rnd 6	Blackpool	(h)	1-2

1953-4

During the close season of 1953 Alex James died. Although the wee Scot's playing days had ended in 1937 he was still part of the Arsenal legend — as indeed were all the members of that great team of the 1930s. His death cast a shadow over Highbury. As the players returned to begin training, everyone felt a keen sense of loss. With Alex James had died a part of Arsenal Football Club.

The season began with a 2-0 defeat at West Brom with Don Roper at outside-right in place of Freddie Cox — gone during the summer to take up a coaching career — and Ben Marden in the number eleven shirt. Joe Mercer, after announcing his impending retirement had decided to play one more season, such was his love of the game, and Bill Dodgin took Daniel's place at centre-half alongside the old fox. It had been Whittaker's hope that young Dodgin would benefit from Mercer and Lionel Smith. But Smith was hurt at the Hawthorns and for the next game at home to Huddersfield a young full-back from Ellesmere Port, Dennis Evans, made his debut. In addition, Ben Marden reported unfit and into the team stepped a sixteen-year-old amateur groundstaff boy, Gerry Ward.

Ward and Evans both had fine debuts and Ward got the ball into the net, only to be adjudged offside. In fact, the game ended in a 0-0 draw and Arsenal were now obviously short of fire-power. Whittaker had already tried to sign Lawrie Reilly, Hibs' unsettled Scotland centre-forward, and Leeds United's John Charles. Crayston saw Charles net four goals against Notts County and was told by Leeds that £40,000 — a staggering amount then — would not buy the brilliant Welshman. Meanwhile, Arsenal's crisis worsened. In the third match of the season they lost 1-0 at Sheffield United which meant three games played and not one goal scored by an Arsenal player. On 29 August Arsenal managed a goal at last when a magnificent effort by Jimmy Logie levelled the scores at Villa Park. But Villa scored again and Arsenal were still without a win.

Things seemed to go from bad to worse. On 12 September Arsenal made the long journey to Sunderland without Tom Whittaker who had gone to Portsmouth to try and sign Jack Froggatt (he had also had thoughts about Leicester's Johnny Morris and Fulham's Bedford Jezzard). George Swindin was playing in his last game for Arsenal at Roker Park and at half-time the Wearsiders were leading 2-1 after Lishman opened the scoring. Then in the second-half they blitzed Arsenal. Poor Swindin's last game, in which he collided with a post and was concussed, saw him let in seven goals. Arsenal crashed 7-1 and the resulting newspaper publicity of Whittaker's journey to Portsmouth killed the Froggatt transfer. After eight games Arsenal's record read: P8, W0, D2, L6, Goals 6-18, Pts 2, Position 22nd.

Cliff Holton scores a superb headed goal against the Brazilian club Portuguesa de Desportos in a friendly at Highbury in February 1954. The unlucky goalkeeper is Padua Mello.

Three days later Arsenal played at Stamford Bridge with Alex Forbes at outside-right and Arthur Shaw playing his first game of the season. Forbes was a success, Shaw played like a lion, and Lishman scored both goals as Arsenal won 2-0. Two days later Whittaker received a bombshell when Brentford's chairman rang him and asked if he would like to buy Tommy Lawton the Bees' thirty-three-year-old international centre-forward. At first Whittaker was undecided—and then he plunged for Lawton who made his debut on 19 September before 65,869 fans at Highbury. Lishman scored two—one from a Lawton pass—and Arsenal drew 2-2. In the next eighteen games Arsenal won ten and drew six times to go from bottom to seventh place. Two weeks after the Lawton signing, Arsenal snapped up Chelsea's unsettled wing-half Bill Dickson.

In the fourth round of the FA Cup there were shocks and sensations when Norwich—a Third Division side—knocked out Arsenal 2-1 at Highbury and Alex Forbes was sent off with Bobby Brennan of the Canaries. On 24 February—just three weeks after Forbes's dismissal—Doug Lishman was sent off at Deepdale to add to Arsenal's uncharacteristic disciplinary problems. On 6 April the midweek visit of Villa drew only 14,519 fans to Highbury, the lowest for years, and four days later at Highbury Barry Town's Derek Tapscott made his debut against Liverpool. But the game is more remembered for the tragic accident to Joe Mercer. Mercer collided with Joe Wade and broke his leg. As they carried him off he raised himself from the stretcher and waved goodbye to Arsenal fans. A superb playing career was over. Mercer had done as much as Alex James to establish the Arsenal as a truly great club.

First Division results 1953-4

	H	A
Aston Villa	1-1	1-2
Blackpool	1-1	2-2
Bolton	4-3	1-3
Burnley	2-5	1-2
Cardiff	1-1	3-0
Charlton	3-3	5-1
Chelsea	1-2	2-0
Huddersfield	0-0	2-2
Liverpool	3-0	2-1
Manchester City	2-2	0-0
Manchester United	3-1	2-2
Middlesbrough	3-1	0-2
Newcastle	2-1	2-5
Portsmouth	3-0	1-1
Preston	3-2	1-0
Sheffield United	1-1	0-1
Sheffield Wednesday	4-1	1-2
Sunderland	1-4	1-7
Tottenham	0-3	4-1
West Brom	2-2	0-2
Wolves	2-3	2-0

Final League Record

P	W	D	L	F	A	Pts	Pos
42	15	13	14	75	73	43	12th

FA Cup

Rnd 3	Aston Villa	(h)	5-1
Rnd 4	Norwich City	(h)	1-2

Derek Tapscott continues his bright start to an Arsenal career by scoring the second of his two goals in the 3-0 win over Portsmouth in April 1954.

1954-5

For almost half the season Arsenal fans feared the worst—that their beloved club would be relegated to the Second Division. After twenty games the Gunners record read: P20, W5, D4, L11, Goals 34-37, Pts 14, Position 19th. Then an amazing revival which started at Christmas sent them soaring up the table to fifth place and only a late lapse—three defeats in the last four games—cost Arsenal players talent money.

The season kicked off on 21 August when Newcastle visited Highbury. Tommy Lawton was suffering from a heavy cold and Cliff Holton donned the number nine shirt in a game which attracted 65,334. But the huge crowd saw the Gunners go down 3-1, and after three matches the club was still looking for its first point, even though Tom Whittaker had made seven changes for the third game at West Brom. Soon questions were being asked as to whether Arsenal's proposed trip to Russia in October was a wise move. The Football League refused the club permission to cancel its game at Leicester on 2 October and the match at Hillsborough one week later.

After drawing 3-3 at Filbert Street the Arsenal party made a horrendous journey to Moscow via Frankfurt, Prague and Minsk before arriving in the Russian capital to play Dynamo on Tuesday 5 October 1954 with the following side: Kelsey, Barnes, Wade, Goring, Dickson, Forbes, Tapscott, Logie, Lawton, Lishman, Roper. Travel-weary Arsenal were beaten 5-0—and the Russians also missed a penalty!

Arsenal players and officials look slightly bemused by the gifts of flowers as they arrive at Vnukovo airport, Moscow, after a horrendous journey for their game with Moscow Dynamo in October 1954.

Yet on the following Saturday, after a round trip of some 3,500 miles, Arsenal defied all the critics and won 2-1 at Hillsborough with the winning goal coming from former Brentford forward, Jimmy Bloomfield. Bloomfield scored on his Arsenal debut with a superb drive from the edge of the penalty area and Arsenal's players forgot their tiredness and the hammering by the Russians. Ten days later Arsenal were in France for their annual match against Racing Club of Paris when Whittaker heard that Aston Villa's graceful wing-half, Danny Blanchflower, was on the move. Immediately the Arsenal boss flew home and made straight for Birmingham where he found the disenchanted Irish international was already the target of Tottenham. Arsenal knew that they would probably have to break the British record to get Blanchflower but they were not prepared to be involved in an auction with their neighbours. Whittaker eventually withdrew and Blanchflower went to White Hart Lane for a reported fee of some £30,000.

The centre-half berth was giving Arsenal some problems. Alex Forbes had played eight games in the number five shirt, Bill Dodgin three, and Bill Dickson three when Dickson went down with appendicitis (this unlucky player had already dislocated his shoulder and injured his knee). Into the side stepped 6ft 4in Jim Fotheringham who had been a junior at Highbury. Fotheringham's first test was a daunting one—up against Bolton's Nat Lofthouse. Arsenal drew that game 2-2 at Burnden Park but were still wallowing when the Christmas games came around.

The Gunners suffered another unhappy game against the Russians—this time Spartak at

Preston's Campbell just beats the lunging foot of Fotheringham. Arsenal won the First Division game 2-0 at Highbury, February 1955.

Highbury—and then beat Chelsea 2-0 at home on Christmas Day and drew 2-2 at Stamford Bridge on 27 December. The Arsenal revival had started. Even a bad fourth round FA Cup result at Wolves did not stop them. Lawton's goal had beaten Cardiff 1-0 at Highbury in the third round but at Molineux the defence was still admiring a spectacular goalmouth clearance by Dennis Evans when Roy Swinbourne nodded home Leslie Smith's quickly taken corner to sink Arsenal 1-0.

Yet in the First Division Arsenal marched on. Between Christmas Day and 11 April their record was sixteen games and eleven wins. They lost only once—at Burnley on 12 February—and won seven games in a row, six of them in succession without conceding a goal. When they went back to Wolves for a League game on 16 April—having just enjoyed a six-point Easter—Arsenal were fifth in the table. At Wolves their run came to an end and they lost 3-1. A 1-1 draw at Bramall Lane two days later was followed by a 3-2 home defeat by Manchester United and a 2-1 defeat at Portsmouth on the last day of the season. Arsenal slipped down to ninth place. In February two internationals had left the club. Arthur Milton, one of the last men to play both soccer and cricket for England, went to Bristol City—where Pat Beasley was manager—and helped them to the Third Division South title. And Jimmy Logie—the man spurned by the Scottish selectors, save for one solitary cap in October 1952—moved to non-League Gravesend.

First Division results 1954-5

	H	A
Aston Villa	2-0	1-2
Blackpool	3-0	2-2
Bolton	3-0	2-2
Burnley	4-0	0-3
Cardiff	2-0	2-1
Charlton	3-1	1-1
Chelsea	1-0	1-1
Everton	2-0	0-1
Huddersfield	3-5	1-0
Leicester	1-1	3-3
Manchester City	2-3	1-2
Manchester United	2-3	1-2
Newcastle	1-3	1-5
Portsmouth	0-1	1-2
Preston	2-0	1-3
Sheffield United	4-0	1-1
Sheffield Wednesday	3-2	2-1
Sunderland	1-3	1-0
Tottenham	2-0	1-0
West Brom	2-2	1-3
Wolves	1-1	1-3

Final League Record

P	W	D	L	F	A	Pts	Pos
42	17	9	16	69	63	43	9th

FA Cup

Rnd 3	Cardiff	(h)	1-0
Rnd 4	Wolves	(a)	0-1

1955-6

Many old faces followed Logie and Milton out of Highbury. In the close season Ben Marden moved to Watford and then Lawton (to Kettering Town as player-manager) and Barnes (to the BBC as a television football consultant) left the great stadium for the last time as players after each appearing in eight games in 1955-6. Young Walsh, a right-winger with just seventeen League games behind him, moved to Cardiff City. And in the spring Joe Wade signed on as player-manager of Hereford United, then in the Southern League, and Doug Lishman went to Nottingham Forest (Lishman's last-ever League game was at Bramall Lane when he scored a hat-trick against Joe Mercer's Sheffield United to clinch First Division football for Forest in 1956-7.

But if old faces were leaving, then there were new ones on the way, both on the field and behind the scenes. Whittaker, concerned by Arsenal's poor start (only one victory in the first nine games), wanted to strengthen the side both up front and at the back. In November he moved for Leyton Orient's star centre-forward, Vic Groves, and Orient's full-back, Stan Charlton. On 8

Tommy Lawton crashes home a perfect knee-high volley, the first of a superb hat-trick as Arsenal beat Cardiff 3-1 in August 1955. But Lawton was soon to leave Highbury to become player-manager of Kettering Town.

September, Whittaker saw Groves score a hat-trick at Colchester as Orient won 6-0 and he knew that this was his man. But it was not until 4 November that Groves and his teammate Charlton joined the Gunners for a joint fee of £30,000. The following day Arsenal grabbed a point at Old Trafford — without Groves — and Whittaker drafted the goalscorer into the side for the following week's game, Sheffield United, at Highbury.

By the middle of March Arsenal were around the danger zone, although there were only ten points between the Gunners (seventeenth in the table) and Blackpool (second). A run of six successive wins from 24 March to 14 April, when they beat Birmingham 1-0 at Highbury, rocketed the Gunners up to fourth place. Only a 2-1 defeat at West Brom in the penultimate match of the season cost Arsenal talent money, and then they only missed out by a fraction of a goal.

Groves scored in Arsenal's 2-1 win but in the next game at Preston he injured his ribs and missed two matches before returning to the side for the West Brom game on 10 December. It was a week later when Dennis Evans scored one of the 'silliest' goals in the history of the Football League. Whittaker gave all his youngsters a chance against star-studded Blackpool. The youngsters responded magnificently and Blackpool were trailing 4-0 when someone in the crowd blew a whistle. Evans thought the game was over — as did everyone

Vic Groves debut goal for Arsenal in the 2-1 win over Sheffield United in November 1955. Groves was bought from Leyton Orient to replace Lawton and soon repaid Whittaker's faith.

else—and thumped the ball jubilantly past Con Sullivan who had turned to pick his cap out of the net. But the referee had not blown and the goal stood—sadly, as Evans had played the great Stan Matthews well all afternoon.

In the FA Cup Arsenal had a fright when little Bedford Town of the Southern League made the journey up to London and pulled back two goals to hold Arsenal to a draw—and very nearly scramble a late equaliser. At Bedford's neat but small ground the following Thursday Arsenal got an even bigger shock when the minnows took the lead. It was not until four minutes from the end that Groves headed a brilliant equaliser and then Tapscott saved Arsenal any further blushes by heading the winner in extra-time after hitting the bar in the dying seconds of normal time. A 4-1 win over Villa and a fine 2-0 victory at Charlton when Groves and Bloomfield scored put Arsenal in the sixth round before they lost 3-1 at home to Birmingham.

Danny Clapton, signed from Leytonstone in August 1953, made the right-wing berth his own in 1955-6, missing only three League games and when Arsenal beat Charlton in the FA Cup he was one of four twenty-two-year-olds in the forward line. Mike Tiddy (twenty-one games) and Gordon Nutt (eight) played after signing from Cardiff City and a new generation of Gunners was taking shape.

On 7 February football was shocked by the announcement that Leyton Orient and former Yeovil manager, Alec Stock, was coming to Arsenal as assistant manager. Arsenal's board had been considering an eventual successor for Whittaker and the manager said that he thought Stock to be the man. But Stock's heart was always at Orient. After fifty-three days he was back at Brisbane Road—though not before Orient chairman Harry Zussman had 'leaked' the story to Bernard Joy, then a journalist with the old London evening paper *The Star*. The story precipitated Stock's decision and he was soon back at the club he loved.

First Division results 1955-6

	H	A
Aston Villa	1-0	1-1
Birmingham	1-0	0-4
Blackpool	4-1	1-3
Bolton	3-1	1-4
Burnley	0-1	1-0
Cardiff	3-1	2-1
Charlton	2-4	0-2
Chelsea	1-1	0-2
Everton	3-2	1-1
Huddersfield	2-0	1-0
Luton	3-0	0-0
Manchester City	0-0	2-2
Manchester United	1-1	1-1
Newcastle	1-0	0-2
Portsmouth	1-3	2-5
Preston	3-2	1-0
Sheffield United	2-1	2-0
Sunderland	3-1	1-3
Tottenham	0-1	1-3
West Brom	2-0	1-2
Wolves	2-2	3-3

Final League Record

P	W	D	L	F	A	Pts	Pos
42	18	10	14	60	61	46	5th

FA Cup

Rnd 3	Bedford Town	(h)	2-2
Replay	Bedford Town	(a)	2-1
Rnd 4	Aston Villa	(h)	4-1
Rnd 5	Charlton	(a)	2-0
Rnd 6	Birmingham	(h)	1-3

1956-7

Arsenal 1956-57. Back row, left to right: R. Swallow, A. Biggs, J. Smailes, H. Dove, R. Greenwood, V Groves. Second row: L. Garrett, B. McGreevey, D. Barrett, E. Cox, D. Bennett, E. Doughty, L. Vernon, D. Bennett. Third row: S. Charlton, J. Fotheringham, P. Goy, C. Sullivan, J. Kelsey, W. Dodgin, D. Herd, D. Tapscott. Front row: D. Clapton, L. Wills, D. Evans, C. Holton, P. Goring, D. Roper, J. Bloomfield, M. Tiddy, G. Nutt. On ground: J. Haverty, J. Barnwell, J. Petts, B. Grough.

The season was overshadowed by the death of Tom Whittaker. At the end of the previous season he collapsed after seeing Arsenal move from nineteenth place to fifth place and only just miss out on collecting talent money. Thirty-seven years of service to Arsenal—during which time he had gone from third team player to secretary-manager—had taken their toll. Whittaker was ordered to rest and this he did in the hope of returning to Highbury soon, though those who visited him knew he was a sick man. His last piece of business for his beloved Gunners was to persuade Vic Groves to re-sign. From his sick bed Whittaker talked to the colourful centre-forward. Highbury fans knew only the Vic Groves who cracked in spectacular goals. Whittaker knew a shy and unassuming Groves. The centre-forward feared he had cartilage trouble and eventually Whittaker's quiet words of confidence talked him into re-signing. A few hours later it was confirmed that the player was to have both cartilages out of his right knee and this he did. His return to the side was not without further bad luck but Vic Groves fought back—no doubt inspired by Whittaker's example—and had a fine career at Highbury.

In October 1956, Tom Whittaker died at the age of fifty-nine. Since 1919 he had served the Gunners as player, trainer, assistant manager and secretary-manager. His contribution to Arsenal was as great as that of Herbert Chapman. Indeed, when one thinks of Arsenal, one always thinks of Chapman *and* Whittaker together. The Arsenal organisation of today owes much to the kindly, dedicated Tom Whittaker. All football mourned his passing.

Arsenal again went to one of their backroom staff and offered the manager's job to Jack Crayston. The former Barrow and Bradford wing-half had made his debut for Arsenal against Liverpool in September 1934 and won a championship medal that season. He added another championship medal in 1937-8 and a Cup winners' medal in 1935-6 as well as being capped for England and after the war was appointed Whittaker's assistant. Now he moved up to take charge of the side and Arsenal separated the secretary-manager's post with Bob Wall taking over the administrative duties.

Arsenal had opened the season with a 0-0 draw at home to Cardiff and then beaten Burnley 2-0 in midweek. When they went 2-0 up at St Andrew's on the second Saturday of the season Arsenal's thoughts began to turn towards a start good enough to launch them into another championship drive. With less than twenty minutes to play the Gunners still held that two-goal advantage and then the Blues hit them four times in quick succession and the game was lost. The first-half of the season continued with plenty of drama. At Burnley on the following Tuesday the Gunners hit the post no less than four times and lost 3-1; and at Portsmouth on 8 September Arsenal stormed into a 2-0 lead, allowed Pompey to draw level, and snatched a winner in the dying seconds through David Herd.

Herd, the son of Scottish international Alex Herd, had signed from Stockport during 1954-5 and after three games that year and five the following season, he claimed a regular spot in the Gunners first team in 1956-7, scoring ten goals in twenty-two games. Little Joe Haverty, signed from an Eire club in 1954, also established a regular place and scored eight goals in twenty-eight games on the left-wing. Dave Bowen, a Welshman from Northampton Town, and Len Willis, a Londoner, were by now familiar names in the Gunners line-up. John Barnwell, Bishop Auckland wing-half, also made his debut.

In the FA Cup a fifth round tie at Preston saw North End centre-half Joe Dunn slice the ball into his own net to help Arsenal to a 3-3 draw; in the Highbury replay Dodgin scored his first first-class

The goal which earned Preston a replay. Thompson side-foots the ball past Con Sullivan to make it 3-3 in the FA Cup fifth round match at Deepdale, February 1957.

goal as the Gunners won 2-1. At West Brom in the quarter-final Wills put through his own goal before Charlton levelled the scores with a forty-yarder. In the replay Holton scored for Arsenal but it was West Brom who went through to the last four.

Still the results see-sawed about. At Wolverhampton on 10 November Arsenal led twice before losing 5-2; two weeks later they were winning 3-0 against Leeds before allowing United to pull back to draw 3-3; and on 15 December the Gunners trailed 2-0 at home to Cardiff for much of the game before winning 3-2. These wildly differing fortunes saw to it that Arsenal finished the season in fifth place—respectable but a massive fourteen points adrift of champions Manchester United.

First Division results 1956-7

	H	A
Aston Villa	2-1	0-0
Birmingham	4-0	2-4
Blackpool	1-1	4-2
Bolton	3-0	1-2
Burnley	2-0	1-3
Cardiff	0-0	3-2
Charlton	3-1	3-1
Chelsea	2-0	1-1
Everton	2-0	0-4
Leeds	1-0	3-3
Luton	1-3	2-1
Manchester City	7-3	3-2
Manchester United	1-2	2-6
Newcastle	0-1	1-3
Portsmouth	1-1	3-2
Preston	1-2	0-3
Sheffield Wednesday	6-3	4-2
Sunderland	1-1	0-1
Tottenham	3-1	3-1
West Brom	4-1	2-0
Wolves	0-0	2-5

FA Cup

Rnd 3	Stoke	(h)	4-1
Rnd 4	Newport	(a)	2-0
Rnd 5	Preston	(a)	3-3
Replay	Preston	(h)	2-1
Rnd 6	West Brom	(a)	2-2
Replay	West Brom	(h)	1-2

Final League Record

P	W	D	L	F	A	Pts	Pos
42	21	8	13	85	69	50	5th

Tapscott scores Arsenal's third goal in the 6-3 First Division win over Sheffield Wednesday at Highbury in February 1957.

1957-8

Arsenal's season was not a good one and yet it will be remembered forever because of one of the most pulsating, superb football matches ever played, a game which also saw the last appearance in England of the ill-fated Busby Babes of Manchester United. Arsenal's season had started with a 1-0 win at Roker Park and a 2-2 draw at home to West Brom which was followed by a 2-0 defeat of Luton at Highbury. There were some thrills on 10 September when Everton won 3-2 at Arsenal Stadium and eleven days later even Clapton's great display at Old Trafford could not stop Manchester United winning 4-2.

Arsenal had a bad Christmas. On Boxing Day they lost 3-0 at Villa Park and two days later Luton Town beat them 4-0 at Kenilworth Road. The third round of the FA Cup paired the Gunners with Third Division South side Northampton Town but even the fact that they had to travel to the County Ground should not have bothered Arsenal, so great was the gulf between the sides. But Arsenal had an all-round off-day. Northampton won the game 3-1, Clapton scoring Arsenal's goal, and for once the Gunners showed an uncharacteristic lack of ability to fight back when the chips were down. The following week Blackpool came to Highbury and beat the Gunners 3-2 and heads were hung low at Highbury. But at this time the side had a Jekyll and Hyde look about it. After this run of depressing defeats they picked themselves up and beat Leicester 1-0 at Filbert Street on 18 January.

Arsenal had no interest in the fourth round of the FA Cup and their next League game was on 1 February when Manchester United came to Highbury to play their last game before flying out to Belgrade for their European Cup-tie with Red Star. By half-time Busby's brilliant young team were coasting 3-0 ahead and everyone on the ground had no reason to suppose other than that Arsenal were in for a thrashing to continue their bad run. After only ten minutes Duncan Edwards drove home from just outside the penalty area, giving Jack Kelsey no chance; on the half-hour Bobby Charlton confirmed his emergence by crashing home Scanlon's cross; and before half-time Tommy Taylor had scored from Morgan's centre.

Yet with half-an-hour to play Arsenal staged an amazing come-back. three goals in less than three minutes pulled them level. First Herd volleyed home Bowen's lob; then Bloomfield scored after Groves had headed Nutt's centre down to his feet; the cheers were still ringing round Highbury when Nutt slung another cross—this time low and hard—and there was Bloomfield diving to head home a breathtaking equaliser. For the next ten minutes Arsenal surged forward looking for what

One of the greatest games of football ever played also marked the last appearance in England of the ill-fated Busby Babes. Bobby Charlton scores Manchester United's second goal in their epic 5-4 win at Highbury just five days before the Munich Air Disaster.

would have been a sensational winner. But United asserted themselves again and Viollet headed the end product of a Charlton-Scanlon move past Kelsey; minutes later it was Taylor making it 5-3 from a seemingly impossible angle. Even then Arsenal refused to lie down and after good work by Bowen and Herd, Tapscott netted Arsenal's fourth.

The crowd had seen a nine-goal thriller and even though Arsenal had ultimately gained nothing from the game, they could be proud to have contributed to such an epic. There could have been no finer epitaph for the brilliant young Manchester United team. In less than a week five of that side, together with many of their colleagues and friends, would be dead, killed in a tangle of twisted aircraft metal in the snow and slush of a Munich runway. Football would never see their like again and it was perhaps fitting that their last game on English soil should be such a thrilling one—and against another of England's most famous clubs, Arsenal. It is worth recording the teams in that historic encounter:

Arsenal: Kelsey, Charlton (S), Evans, Ward, Fotheringham, Bowen, Groves, Tapscott, Herd, Bloomfield, Nutt.

Manchester United: Gregg, Foulkes, Byrne, Colman, Jones, Edwards, Morgans, Charlton (R), Taylor, Viollet, Scanlon.

First Division results 1957-8

	H	A
Aston Villa	4-0	0-3
Birmingham	1-3	1-4
Blackpool	2-3	0-1
Bolton	1-2	1-0
Burnley	0-0	1-2
Chelsea	5-4	0-0
Everton	2-3	2-2
Leeds	2-1	0-2
Leicester	3-1	1-0
Luton	2-0	0-4
Manchester City	2-1	4-2
Manchester United	4-5	2-4
Newcastle	2-3	3-3
Nottingham Forest	1-1	0-4
Portsmouth	3-2	4-5
Preston	4-2	0-3
Sheffield Wednesday	1-0	0-2
Sunderland	3-0	1-0
Tottenham	4-4	1-3
West Brom	2-2	2-1
Wolves	0-2	2-1

Final League Record

P	W	D	L	F	A	Pts	Pos
42	16	7	19	73	85	39	12th

FA Cup

Rnd 3	Northampton	(a)	1-3

Manchester City's German goalkeeper Bert Trautmann lunges at the ball while Tapscott and Herd (Arsenal) and Leivers and Sear (City) can only look on in horror. Arsenal won 2-1, November 1957.

1958-9

Sheffield United's Simpson about to score his first minute goal in the FA Cup fifth round match at Highbury in February 1959. Arsenal recovered to draw 2-2.

In the close season Arsenal found themselves looking for a new manager when Jack Crayston resigned, thus ending a long association with the club. After speculation that Joe Mercer, then managing Sheffield United, would return to Highbury as boss, the club went for another 'old boy' in George Swindin, their former goalkeeper who had gone to Midland League Peterborough and transformed them into one of the best-known non-League clubs in the country.

There were many comings and goings on the field at Highbury during 1958-9. Into the side came Tommy Docherty, Preston North End's Scottish international wing-half, who signed in August; and Wolves and former Portsmouth outside-left Jackie Henderson who joined Arsenal a month later and scored twice on his debut in the 4-3 win over West Brom at Highbury in early October. During the season Len Julians signed and played ten matches. Early in 1958-9 Tapscott (to Cardiff), Holton (to Watford) and Charlton (back to Leyton) all left Highbury and at the season's end Fotheringham, who had been unable to budge Dodgin from the centre-half spot, moved to Hearts while Dave Bowen, after suffering a long spell of injury, went to Northampton Town as player-manager.

Gerry Ward, who had made his debut as a sixteen-year-old left-winger in 1953, but who never maintained a place in the side, had been converted to wing-half and played his first game there in the epic against Manchester United at Highbury the previous season. He played so well that he maintained his place and in 1958-9 appeared thirty-one times. After six matches Arsenal were top of the table as the heaviest-scoring team in the First Division. At the half-way stage they were still top and if it had not been for a bad December—which included a 6-3 defeat at Luton—Arsenal might have taken the title. Even then their recovery might have given the Gunners top place but for injuries to key players at crucial times. In the end they finished third, their highest spot since the championship season of 1952-3.

On 26 November 1958 Jack Kelsey had the unique experience of playing in two top class games on the same day. In the afternoon he helped Wales to a 2-2 draw against England at Villa Park—a game in which Clapton and Bowen also played—and then made a car dash to Highbury to play the full ninety minutes of Arsenal's prestige friendly with Italian Champions, Juventus. Clapton, too, travelled back and after thirty-seven minutes he came on as a substitute for Gordon Nutt.

Reserves John Petts, John Barnwell and Roy Gouldon—son of former England, West Ham and Chelsea inside-forward Len Gouldon—also played. Barnwell and Gouldon, who came on as substitute, both scored and fifteen minutes from the end Jimmy Bloomfield put the result beyond doubt after the great Italian side had taken the lead through John Charles after five minutes. With Groves, Herd and Ward all injured and unable to play, it had been a fine win for Arsenal's young side. Besides Clapton's England debut, Herd also played international soccer for the first time and when Scotland played Wales, Arsenal supplied five players, Herd, Docherty, Henderson (for Scotland) and Kelsey and Bowen (for Wales).

Arsenal suffered many injuries during the season. Herd, Bowen, Henderson, Ward, Groves and Wills were all sidelined for long periods and disaster struck Kelsey in the fifth round FA Cup replay at Bramall Lane. The Welshman broke his arm and Arsenal lost 3-0. Jim Standen performed brilliantly as Kelsey's replacement, particularly in the 1-1 draw at West Brom on 21 February when injuries to Henderson, Groves and Wills reduced the Gunners to eight fit men. A string of superb saves saved Arsenal that day and then Standen was himself injured and missed the next match at home to Leeds when third-choice Goy did well as Arsenal won 1-0.

First Division results 1958-9

	H	A
Aston Villa	1-2	2-1
Birmingham	2-1	1-4
Blackburn	1-1	2-4
Blackpool	1-4	2-1
Bolton	6-1	1-2
Burnley	3-0	1-3
Chelsea	1-1	3-0
Everton	3-1	6-1
Leeds	1-0	1-2
Leicester	5-1	3-2
Luton	1-0	3-6
Manchester City	4-1	0-0
Manchester United	3-2	1-1
Newcastle	3-2	0-1
Nottingham Forest	3-1	1-1
Portsmouth	5-2	1-0
Preston	1-2	1-2
Tottenham	3-1	4-1
West Brom	4-3	1-1
West Ham	1-2	0-0
Wolves	1-1	1-6

Final League Record

P	W	D	L	F	A	Pts	Pos
42	21	8	13	88	68	50	3rd

FA Cup

Rnd 3	Bury	(a)	1-0
Rnd 4	Colchester	(a)	2-2
Replay	Colchester	(h)	4-0
Rnd 5	Sheffield United	(h)	2-2
Replay	Sheffield United	(a)	0-3

Arsenal's latest signing, centre-forward Len Julians, jumps high to avoid a collision with Luton's Ron Baynham in December 1958. Arsenal won 1-0.

1959-60

Another season of early opportunity marred by a long injury list. After completing a quarter of their matches Arsenal were lying a handy fourth behind Spurs, Wolves and Burnley. Arsenal opened the season with a shock 1-0 home defeat at the hands of newly-promoted Sheffield Wednesday. Yet this was to be one of the Gunners' only two defeats in the first eleven matches. In the first midweek match they hammered Forest 3-0 at the City Ground and then got a point in the 3-3 draw at Wolverhampton on the second Saturday of the season.

In those first eleven games Herd and Danny Clapton had each scored six goals to establish themselves as marksmen to watch out for in 1959-60 and even Dennis Evans's ankle injury — he chipped a bone — and the fact that Mel Charles (signed from Swansea Town) had cartilage trouble, could not take away Arsenal's confidence in that first quarter of the season. But the run did not last for much longer. On 17 October Tommy Docherty broke his ankle when his old club Preston came to Highbury. Preston took full advantage of the ten-men Gunners and won 3-0.

By the time Docherty was fit enough to resume his place in the Arsenal team in January, the Gunners had slipped from fourth place right down to sixteenth. There was a superb performance at Stamford Bridge on 21 November when Chelsea were beaten 3-1, but this was followed by a run of five defeats, during which time Arsenal conceded twenty goals. On 28 November West Brom won 4-2 at Highbury, then followed defeats at Newcastle (1-4), at home to Burnley (2-4), away to Shef-field Wednesday (1-5) and at home to Luton (0-3 on Boxing Day). The defeat by the Hatters was Arsenal's fourth successive home loss.

The FA Cup pitted Arsenal against Second Division Rotherham United at Millmoor, just a week after Wolves had drawn 4-4 at Highbury. Clearly, the Arsenal defence was suspect. In the Millmoor tie only an own goal by a Rotherham defender saved Arsenal's blushes. The replay at Highbury on the following Wednesday saw United earn a creditable 1-1 draw (Bloomfield scored for Arsenal); and in the second replay at Hillsborough five days later — Arsenal had lost 3-0 at Spurs in the meantime — United finally finished the job with an emphatic 2-0 win.

There were some brighter moments to follow. Mel Charles scored a hat-trick against Blackburn on 6 February — Arsenal's first home win since 31 October — and collected eight goals in nine games from centre-forward. Jimmy Bloomfield netted three when Manchester United were beaten 5-2 at Highbury on 23 April. This was the third hat-trick by an Arsenal player that season. In that second match of the season win at Forest, Danny Clapton had bagged all three goals — the first hat-trick by an Arsenal winger since Ben Marden's three against Charlton in 1953-4.

The injuries continued to mount up. Clapton had a cartilage operation and Evans, only three games into his comeback from a broken ankle, had the misfortune to break the other ankle. The only consolation was that these injuries helped young players like Magill, Sneddon, Dennis Clapton and Everitt to be blooded in the Arsenal first team.

Jimmy Bloomfield draws first blood for the Gunners five minutes into the game with West Ham at Highbury on 14 November 1959. But the Hammers hit back to win 3-1 and go top of the First Division.

First Division results 1959-60

	H	A
Blackburn	5-2	1-1
Blackpool	2-1	1-2
Birmingham	3-0	0-3
Bolton	2-1	1-0
Burnley	2-4	2-3
Chelsea	1-4	3-1
Everton	2-1	1-3
Fulham	2-0	0-3
Leeds	1-1	2-3
Leicester	1-1	2-2
Luton	0-3	1-0
Manchester City	3-1	2-1
Manchester United	5-2	2-4
Newcastle	1-0	1-4
Nottingham Forest	1-1	3-0
Preston	0-3	3-0
Sheffield Wednesday	0-1	1-5
Tottenham	1-1	0-3
West Brom	2-4	0-1
West Ham	1-3	0-0
Wolves	4-4	3-3

Arsenal 1959-60. Back row, left to right:
J. Henderson, W. McCullough, W. Dodgin,
J. Kelsey, J. Standen, M. Charles, D. Evans,
L. Julians. Front row: D. R. Clapton, G. Ward,
L. Wills, V. Groves, T. Docherty, J. Bloomfield,
D. Herd. On ground: J. Barnwell, J. Haverty.

Final League Record

P	W	D	L	F	A	Pts	Pos
42	15	9	18	68	80	39	13th

FA Cup

Rnd 3	Rotherham	(a)	2-2
Replay	Rotherham	(h)	1-1
Replay	Rotherham	(n)	0-2

n = neutral

One week later and Bloomfield scores again. This time his goal put Arsenal 2-0 up against Chelsea. The Gunners stormed to a 3-0 lead after twenty-eight minutes and Chelsea could only reply once in the second half.

1960-1

Arsenal's endeavours on the field were largely overshadowed by the comings and goings off it during 1960-1. Several new players arrived at Highbury—including one whose story made the news pages rather than the sports pages of the daily papers—while several more left the club. Those on the way out included Standen, who was transferred to Luton Town in October, Bill Dodgin, who returned to Fulham without playing a first team game in 1960-1, Tommy Docherty, signed by Chelsea as coach, Gordon Nutt, who went to Southend, Jimmy Bloomfield, off to Birmingham in November, and Everitt moved to Northampton. In addition, former Chelsea and Brentford half-back, Ron Greenwood, who had joined the Highbury coaching staff in December 1957, went to West Ham. At the end of the previous season trainer Billy Milne had retired after thirty-seven years at the club.

Coming in to Highbury were George Eastham, Newcastle United's unsettled inside-forward who was in the middle of a legal battle to win his freedom from the North-East club, and two more inside-men, Arfon Griffiths from Wrexham, who came in February, and Peter Kane from Northampton. Another new arrival was Glentoran's goalkeeper John McClelland. In addition, several youngsters on the staff got their first chance in 1960-1, including Dave Bacuzzi, Terry Neill, Alan Skirton and Geoff Strong. Among other youngsters waiting in the wings were Peter Simpson, signed from Gorleston in May 1960, David Court, who came straight from school in April 1959, and Jon Sammels, who came from Suffolk on 5 January 1961—'I'll never forget that date!' he maintains to this day.

The season was also overshadowed by Arsenal's North London neighbours Spurs who were taking football by storm and powering their way to the first League and Cup 'Double' this century—Arsenal's turn would come a decade later. At one time it looked as though the Gunners thirty-year-old record of sixty-six First Division points would be eclipsed by Tottenham but in the end they fell just short, although Arsenal now had to share their proud record. Spurs broke Arsenal's record of twenty-eight wins in a season—by three—but in their record-breaking year of 1930-1, Arsenal lost only four games whereas Tottenham went down seven times—although they did do the double over the Gunners, winning 3-2 at Highbury and 4-2 at White Hart Lane.

While Spurs were marching on, Arsenal opened their own season with a 3-2 away defeat at the hands of Burnley. A 1-0 midweek win over Preston at Highbury was followed by a 3-0 beating of Nottingham Forest at home on the second Saturday of the season and at last the Gunners settled down. Arsenal stayed around the top eight in the First Division for a long time. On 10 December at Highbury, George Eastham made his debut after his £47,500 move from Newcastle. Eastham's first game in an Arsenal first team shirt was against his father's old club Bolton Wanderers. Arsenal won 5-1 and Eastham bagged the last two goals. Christmas brought two 1-1 draws with Sheffield Wednesday and on New Year's Eve the Gunners started their celebrations

Jack Kelsey makes a brilliant save from Burnley's Pointer, with Sneddon, the Gunners centre-half, watching anxiously in December 1960. But Burnley beat the Arsenal goalkeeper five times to maintain their challenge for the title.

with a magnificent 5-3 win at Nottingham Forest to complete a double over the Trentside club.

On 7 January Arsenal hauled themselves up to Roker Park for the third round of the FA Cup but lost 2-1 and a week later it was back to League action and a 5-4 win over Manchester City at Highbury. Sadly, Arsenal won only two of their last twelve games and slipped to eleventh place when the final tables were drawn up. Despite the fact that David Herd finished leading scorer with twenty-nine goals, including four hat-tricks — the best individual season's figures since Ronnie Rookes thirty-three in 1947-8 — Arsenal fell down on many occasions through lack of penetration. In more than half the League games Arsenal's forwards could manage no more than a goal a game, while at the back, the defenders conceded four or more goals no less than eight times.

First Division results 1960-1

	H	A
Aston Villa	2-1	2-2
Birmingham	2-0	0-2
Blackburn	0-0	4-2
Blackpool	1-0	1-1
Bolton	5-1	1-1
Burnley	2-5	2-3
Cardiff	2-3	0-1
Chelsea	1-4	1-3
Everton	3-2	1-4
Fulham	4-2	2-2
Leicester	1-3	1-2
Manchester City	5-4	0-0
Manchester United	2-1	1-1
Newcastle	5-0	3-3
Nottingham Forest	3-0	5-3
Preston	1-0	0-2
Sheffield Wednesday	1-1	1-1
Tottenham	2-3	2-4
West Brom	1-0	3-2
West Ham	0-0	0-6
Wolves	1-5	3-5

Final League Record

P	W	D	L	F	A	Pts	Pos
42	15	11	16	77	85	41	11th

FA Cup

Rnd 3	Sunderland	(a)	1-2

This time Kelsey is beaten as Leicester's Appleton cracks home a goal at Highbury in February 1961. Again Arsenal went down.

1961-2

Arsenal started the season with two new players in Northampton Town's Laurie Brown and Hibernian's John MacLeod. Brown, a former amateur international centre-half, played in all but one of the Gunners' League matches while MacLeod, who had played outside-right in Scotland's last four internationals of the previous season, turned out thirty-seven times for Arsenal. In November Arsenal signed another internationl in Wolverhampton Wanderer's wing-half, Eddie Clamp. Clamp played in eighteen matches as the Gunners finished the season in tenth place with Alan Skirton leading the League scorers with nineteen goals in thirty-eight appearances. Skirton's success was particularly pleasing. He signed for Arsenal from Bath City in January 1959 when he was still doing his National Service and a serious illness delayed his League debut for the Gunners until 1960-1. Now the youngster had held his place in the side with some fine performances.

Two more youngsters who made their first appearances in 1961-2 were George Armstrong, signed as a trailist from County Durham in August 1961, and goalkeeper Ian McKechnie. Armstrong was signed as an inside-forward but during the trial matches he was switched to the wing with such success that George Swindin signed him as a professional in August 1961 and played him in the first team in four League games that season. McKechnie's transformation was even more unusual. He came as an outside-left but after Swindin watched him in goal during a kickabout he moved the Dumbartonshire youngster between the posts where he made three League appearances in 1961-2.

But there was a much sadder side to the season. At the end of it, Jack Kelsey, the Gunners' Welsh international goalkeeper and their most experienced player, injured his back in an international in Sao Paulo in May and was forced out of the game. Kelsey was playing his forty-first game for Wales when the Brazilian centre-forward Vava crashed into him fifteen minutes after half-time. For thirty-three-year-old Kelsey it was the end of his career. Although he dismissed the injury as just another knock, Kelsey found that after two or three minutes he could not move a limb. After trying to take a back pass from Stuart Williams, Kelsey had to be taken off. It was his last game of soccer. Despite months of painful treatment, during which time he was put in a wire cage, the great Welsh keeper was told that he would never play again. To add a touch of bitter irony to the situation, Kelsey was told that his career had ended on 21 November 1962 — the day he should have been playing for Wales against England at Wembley.

It was the end of a superb career. In 327 League appearances for the Gunners Kelsey had shown himself to be one of the most courageous goalkeepers in post-war soccer. Besides diving fearlessly at the feet of any forward, Jack Kelsey also built up his own private store of knowledge about individual opponent's habits. Thus, he would know which foot a player favoured, which side a penalty-taker liked to aim for, and many more facts which made him that bit more efficient between Arsenal's posts. Happily, Jack Kelsey was not lost to the club and today he is manager of Arsenal's promotions office and Gunners Shop, working in the very heart of his beloved Highbury.

Billy Wright, the former Wolves and England star, pictured at his desk on the day he took over as manager of Arsenal in May 1962.

First Division results 1961-2

	H	A
Aston Villa	4-5	1-3
Birmingham	1-1	0-1
Blackburn	0-0	0-0
Blackpool	3-0	1-0
Bolton	1-2	1-2
Burnley	2-2	2-0
Cardiff	1-1	1-1
Chelsea	0-3	3-2
Everton	2-3	1-4
Fulham	1-0	2-5
Ipswich	0-3	2-2
Leicester	4-4	1-0
Manchester City	3-0	2-3
Manchester United	5-1	3-2
Nottingham Forest	2-1	1-0
Sheffield United	2-0	1-2
Sheffield Wednesday	1-0	1-1
Tottenham	2-1	3-4
West Brom	0-1	0-4
West Ham	2-2	3-3
Wolves	3-1	3-2

Final League Record

P	W	D	L	F	A	Pts	Pos
42	16	11	15	71	72	43	10th

FA Cup

Rnd 3	Bradford City	(h)	3-0
Rnd 4	Manchester United	(a)	0-1

1962-3

Just as the previous season had seen the demise of one great and brave Arsenal keeper, so too another former Gunners goalie left the club when George Swindin was replaced as manager. Swindin's stern disciplinary measures upset individual players and for the start of 1962-3 former England and Wolves centre-half Billy Wright was installed as manager at Highbury. His appointment caused a few raised eyebrows for it was the first time in years that Arsenal had gone outside the club for a manager. But Wright's playing record—a record 105 caps for England—was impeccable and his reputation soon attracted young talent to the club. His first big signing was Joe Baker from Torino for some £70,000. Baker had been unhappy in Italy since his transfer from Hibernian and the Liverpool-born player—who played for England with a thick Scottish accent—was glad to take up Wright's offer to join Arsenal.

The Gunners finished the season in seventh place and Baker repaid a large lump of his transfer fee with twenty-nine goals from thirty-nine appearances. In goal John McClelland now had his chance after the unfortunate injury to Kelsey and when he missed nine games between the posts, young Ian McKechnie stepped up. Arsenal also signed two young goalkeepers on during the season when John Black became a full-time professional in February 1963 after joining Arsenal as an apprentice; and Tonbridge's amateur Tony Burns signed professional forms a month later.

Fred Clarke, a young defender from Glenavon—McClelland's old club—who made his debut at the end of 1961-2, played five times in Arsenal's League side; and left-winger Terry Anderson and half-back Rod Smithson—both former apprentices at Arsenal—made their League debuts. The Gunners figured in some high-scoring games in the season. They drew 5-5 at Blackburn on 3 November, one week after beating Wolves 5-4 at Highbury. And at the beginning of October, in the North London 'derby' at White Hart Lane, Arsenal had shared eight goals with Spurs. Geoff Strong gave Baker good support, finishing second-highest scorer with eighteen goals, and Alan Skirton continued his good work with ten goals in twenty-eight appearances.

But although Arsenal's first team took no honours during the season, the club's reserves and

Jack Kelsey has his hands full. A great career was ended by injury.

junior strength was apparent,. The Football Combination (Saturday Section), the Metropolitan League, and the London FA Challenge Cup all found their way to the Highbury trophy shelf in 1962-3. Members of the Gunners' reserve strength included Peter Storey, Peter Simpson, and Ray Bloomfield, nephew of Arsenal's former star, Jimmy Bloomfield. Billy Wright consolidated the club's position in his first season, improving their League position by three places and steering them into the fifth round of the FA Cup before Liverpool won 2-1 at Highbury.

Final League Record

P	W	D	L	F	A	Pts	Pos
42	18	10	14	86	77	46	7th

FA Cup

Rnd 3	Oxford	(h)	5-1
Rnd 4	Sheffield Wednesday	(h)	2-0
Rnd 5	Liverpool	(h)	1-2

Billy McCullough, signed from Portadown in September 1958, who played in all forty-two of Arsenal's First Division games in 1962-3.

Terry Neill, another signing from Irish soccer, who played seventeen times in 1962-3, bringing his total league appearances for Arsenal to fifty-one. One day he would return to Highbury as manager.

John Barnwell, another Arsenal player who would find fame as a manager.

First Division results 1962-3

	H	A
Aston Villa	1-2	1-3
Birmingham	2-0	2-2
Blackburn	3-1	5-5
Blackpool	2-0	2-3
Bolton	3-2	0-3
Burnley	2-3	1-2
Everton	4-3	1-1
Fulham	3-0	3-1
Ipswich	3-1	1-1
Leicester	1-1	0-2
Liverpool	2-2	1-2
Manchester City	2-3	4-2
Manchester United	1-3	3-2
Nottingham Forest	0-0	0-3
Leyton Orient	2-0	2-1
Sheffield United	1-0	3-3
Sheffield Wednesday	1-2	3-2
Tottenham	2-3	4-4
West Brom	3-2	2-1
West Ham	1-1	4-0
Wolves	5-4	0-1

1963-4

Billy Wright made another big early-season signing for Arsenal when he flew to Scotland and came back with the signature of Dundee's big centre-half, Ian Ure, for £62,500. News of Ure's availability reached Wright when he was on tour with the side in the Dutch town of Enschede. A board meeting of Arsenal directors was held in the team's hotel and an offer sent to Bob Shankly (brother of Liverpool's Bill), the manager of Dundee, by telegram. Shankly accepted Arsenal's offer and on return from the tour, Wright and Bob Wall flew to Scotland to secure the big man. Ure missed only one game in his first season and until his transfer to Manchester United in August 1969 he gave the Gunners valuable service.

Early in the season McClelland broke his arm and this gave another chance to young Ian McKechnie, who played in eleven games, and Bob Wilson, an amateur who turned professional in March 1964 and who played five times after abandoning a career as a PE teacher in favour of full-time soccer. But Arsenal desperately needed an experienced goalkeeper and in November 1963 they signed Liverpool and former Burnley player Jim Furnell. Furnell, a native of Manchester, played regularly for the rest of the season, making twenty-one appearances. Another player to make his debut for Arsenal in 1963-4 was John Radford, who came from Pontefract, Yorkshire, as an apprentice in October 1962, becoming a full-time professional in February 1964.

Up front Joe Baker again led the League scorers with twenty-six goals from thirty-nine games while Geoff Strong weighed in with twenty-six to give him valuable support. In the FA Cup Arsenal—who slipped a place in the League from the previous season—again went out to Liverpool in the fifth round. Their Cup run had started with an easy 5-1 win over Fourth Division minnows, Oxford, comparative Football League newcomers. Then sixth-placed Sheffield Wednesday from the First Division were beaten 2-0 before Liverpool came to Highbury on 16 March and for the second successive year ended Arsenal's hopes of their first major honour since 1953.

But there was the experience of European football in 1963-4 as Arsenal went into battle in the Fairs Cup. In the first round Arsenal faced the little Danish team of Staevnet and won 7-1 away from home with goals from Strong and Baker, who each scored hat-tricks, and MacLeod. In the return leg the Danish side sprang a surprise by beating Arsenal 3-2, goals from Skirton and Barnwell giving the Gunners a 9-4 aggregate and a second round tie with the Belgian club Liege. In the first leg at Highbury young Terry Anderson netted in Arsenal's 1-1 draw; but the result was not enough to save them in Belgium and the Gunners went down 3-1 with Billy McCullough grabbing their goal. It was Arsenal's first taste of European competition and it ended in dismal failure.

George Eastham hits the Wolves bar at Highbury in August 1963.

First Division results 1963-4

	H	A
Aston Villa	3-0	1-2
Birmingham	4-1	4-1
Blackburn	0-0	1-4
Blackpool	5-3	1-0
Bolton	4-3	1-1
Burnley	3-2	3-0
Chelsea	2-4	1-3
Everton	6-0	1-2
Fulham	2-2	4-1
Ipswich	6-0	2-1
Leicester	0-1	2-7
Liverpool	1-1	0-5
Manchester United	2-1	1-3
Nottingham Forest	4-2	0-2
Sheffield United	1-3	2-2
Sheffield Wednesday	1-1	4-0
Stoke	1-1	2-1
Tottenham	4-4	1-3
West Brom	3-2	0-4
West Ham	3-3	1-1
Wolves	1-3	2-2

At the other end it's Arsenal's turn to have a lucky escape as new signing Ian Ure — playing his first game after moving from Dundee — watches Farmer's shot hit the post.

Final League Record

P	W	D	L	F	A	Pts	Pos
42	17	11	14	90	82	45	8th

FA Cup

Rnd 3	Wolves	(h)	2-1
Rnd 4	West Brom	(a)	3-3
Replay	West Brom	(h)	2-0
Rnd 5	Liverpool	(h)	0-1

Fairs Cup

Rnd 1,	1st leg	Staevnet	(a)	7-1
Rnd 1,	2nd leg	Staevnet	(h)	2-3
Rnd 2,	1st leg	Liege	(h)	1-1
Rnd 2,	2nd leg	Liege	(a)	1-3

This time the ball finds the back of the net. Farmer raises his arms as Hinton's shot beats McClelland. Wolves went on to win 3-1.

1964-5

West Bromwich Albion's England international full-back, Don Howe, signed for Arsenal in April 1964 just before the club embarked on a tour of South Africa and he missed only two League games in 1964-5 in what was Arsenal's worst season for five years when they finished thirteenth in the First Division and were knocked out of the FA Cup by Peterborough United. In a bid to pick up Arsenal's fortunes, Billy Wright plunged into the transfer market in October 1964 when he brought Leicester City's Scottish international half-back Frank McLintock from the Midlanders for an Arsenal record fee of £80,000.

McLintock soon settled into the Gunners side and he was to stay there for several seasons, prompting and leading the side to the glory of the 'Double' in 1971. But in 1964-5 those golden times were still some way away and there was no one at Highbury who could be thinking of such things as the Gunners struggled to find their true form. In goal young Tony Burns made his debut and was sufficiently impressive to turn out in twenty-four League games in his first League season. Another youngster making his first appearance in the League was Tommy Baldwin, who had been on Arsenal's books since December 1962. Peter Simpson, who made his debut the previous year, also managed six games and the future at least looked promising with so many potentially good players on the books.

But the immediate results were far from encouraging. In the First Division Arsenal managed less than one point per game and lost five games at Highbury. Although the side were in no danger of leaving the First Division, the tempo of the season

Arsenal 1964-5. Back row, left to right: G. Strong, G. Ferry, A. Skirton, D. Howe, R. Wilson, J. Furnell, J. Snedden, I. Ure, P. Simpson, T. Neill. Front row: J. Magill, T. Anderson, F. Clarke, J. Baker, G. Eastham, D. Court, W. McCullough, G. Armstrong, J. Sammels.

was one of mediocrity, something with which football fans all over the country had not associated Arsenal for over thirty years. But if the League programme gave the Gunners little joy, then the returns from the FA Cup filled them with gloom. In the third round Arsenal managed a 2-0 win at lowly Darlington, struggling near the foot of the Fourth Division, before Peterborough United entertained the Gunners at their London Road ground on 30 January 1965 for an intriguing fourth round tie.

Peterborough were already FA Cup giantkillers from their Midland League days. Moreover they were the club to which George Swindin had gone as player-manager when he left Arsenal as a player and before he returned to Highbury as manager. Peterborough—or Posh as they are known—won the Fourth Division title in their first-ever season in the Football League in 1960-1 and despite their comparatively lowly status were one of the best-known clubs in the country, particularly when the FA Cup came round. On that January day their ground was packed to capacity and the fans were not disappointed. Peterborough beat the Gunners 2-1 to add another scalp to their giantkilling belt. It was another dark moment for Arsenal Football Club—once proud champions of all they surveyed, now struggling to recapture those golden days.

First Division results 1964-5

	H	A
Aston Villa	3-1	1-3
Birmingham	3-0	3-2
Blackburn	1-1	2-1
Blackpool	3-1	1-1
Burnley	3-2	1-2
Chelsea	1-3	1-2
Everton	3-1	0-1
Fulham	2-0	4-3
Leeds	1-2	1-3
Leicester	4-3	3-2
Liverpool	0-0	2-3
Manchester United	2-3	1-3
Nottingham Forest	0-3	0-3
Sheffield United	1-1	0-4
Sheffield Wednesday	1-1	1-2
Stoke	3-2	1-4
Sunderland	3-1	2-0
Tottenham	3-1	1-3
West Brom	1-1	0-0
West Ham	0-3	1-2
Wolves	4-1	1-0

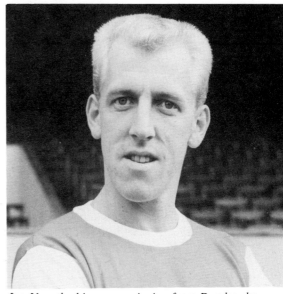

Ian Ure, the big money signing from Dundee, he brought his league tally up to eighty-four games.

Final League Record

P	W	D	L	F	A	Pts	Pos
42	17	7	18	69	75	41	13th

FA Cup

Rnd 3	Darlington	(a)	2-0
Rnd 4	Peterborough	(a)	1-2

George Eastham is convinced that he has scored — but the ball is somewhere in the Craven Cottage mud. Fulham defenders Brown, Keetch and Langley are all on the goal-line. Arsenal's McLintock and Fulham's Howfield look on, December 1964. Arsenal won a thriller 4-3.

1965-6

One of the most dismal nights in the story of Arsenal Football Club was on Thursday 5 May 1966 when a paltry 4,554 turned up to scatter themselves around Arsenal Stadium—scene of so many great matches—to watch the Gunners go down 3-0 to Leeds United in the penultimate match of the 1965-6 season. Admittedly, fixture congestion meant that the game had to be played that night in direct opposition to the televised European Cup-winners' Cup Final between Liverpool and Borussia Dortmund at Hampden Park, but nevertheless such a crowd at Highbury was unthinkable. It was the culmination of a poor season for the Gunners, fourteenth in the First Division and knocked out of the FA Cup at the first hurdle. Changes had to be made and Arsenal would soon have a new manager.

The season had opened with a 2-1 win at home to Stoke City with Joe Baker netting both the Gunners' goals. There followed a strange encounter for Arsenal—an away First Division match at Northampton Town. Northampton were in their first—and, as it happened, last—season in the top flight but Arsenal could only manage a 1-1 draw on a ground also used by Northamptonshire County Cricket Club when Tommy Baldwin scored. Chelsea won 3-1 at Highbury on the third Saturday of the season and the Gunners' only real ray of sunshine before Christmas was a 6-2 win at home to Sheffield United on 6 November when Armstrong, Baker and Skirton each scored twice.

The Christmas games with Sheffield Wednesday produced contrasting results. At Hillsborough on 27 December, Arsenal lost 4-0; the following day at Highbury, Eastham (two), Skirton, Sammels and Baker helped the Gunners to a 5-2 win. Then Arsenal lost three League games on the trot (0-1 to Fulham, 0-1 to Liverpool, and 1-2 to Blackburn Rovers) followed by a 3-0 FA Cup third round defeat at Blackburn one week later. It had been a black start to 1966 for Arsenal and for Joe Baker it was the end of his Highbury career. He moved to Nottingham Forest for £60,000 after scoring thirteen goals in twenty-four matches in 1965-6 to finish the season as Arsenal's top scorer, despite the fact that he left with just over half the season gone. Altogether Baker had scored exactly 100 goals in League, FA Cup and Fairs Cup matches.

Arsenal's season dragged on and ended in yet another disappointing climax for the club which had not won a major honour for thirteen seasons. Not since the 1920s had the club gone so long

unrewarded. During the early part of the close season the Board met and discussed the position of manager Billy Wright. It was inevitable that the former Wolves and England star would go and he took the decision like the gentleman he is. Yet, although Wright brought no honours to the club, he did bring on many fine players, including several who would appear in the 'Double' season. Peter Storey was just one. Storey signed as an apprentice for George Swindin in May 1961 and under Wright's management he was given his first chance in 1965-6 when he came into the side and played twenty-eight games.

John Radford, Pat Rice, Bob Wilson and Sammy Nelson all joined Arsenal as youngsters under Wright; and McLintock, Ure, and Baker were big money signings who succeeded at the club. Besides Storey, other young players who made their debuts in 1965-6 were Jimmy McGill, Gordon Neilson and John Walley, while Billy McCullough left the club after playing 253 League games. Don Howe had the misfortune to break his leg in March and David Court, a man becoming something of a utility player, stepped into the right-back spot and, along with Storey, proved an able deputy for the injured defender.

George Armstrong, Arsenal's England under-23 international who played thirty-nine league games in 1965-6, together with Terry Neill, more than any other player.

John Radford played thirty-two league games to establish himself in the Gunners first team.

First Division results 1965-6

	H	A
Aston Villa	3-3	0-3
Blackburn	2-2	1-2
Blackpool	0-0	3-5
Burnley	1-1	2-2
Chelsea	1-3	0-0
Everton	0-1	1-3
Fulham	2-1	0-1
Leeds	0-3	0-2
Leicester	1-0	1-3
Liverpool	0-1	2-4
Manchester United	4-2	1-2
Newcastle	1-3	1-0
Northampton	1-1	1-1
Nottingham Forest	1-0	1-0
Sheffield United	6-2	0-3
Sheffield Wednesday	5-2	0-4
Stoke	2-1	3-1
Sunderland	1-1	2-0
Tottenham	1-1	2-2
West Brom	1-1	4-4
West Ham	3-2	1-2

Final League Record

P	W	D	L	F	A	Pts	Pos
42	12	13	17	62	75	37	14th

FA Cup

Rnd 3	Blackburn	(a)	0-3

1966-7

Bertie Mee, Arsenal's new manager for 1966-7.

On 20 June 1966 Arsenal's physiotherapist and trainer, Bertie Mee, took over as acting manager in place of Billy Wright. The promotion of Mee from treatment room to manager's office at Highbury was similar to that of Tom Whittaker some nineteen years earlier when he had taken over from George Allison—although Allison retired while Wright was relieved of his position after some dark days at the club. Mee, a former Derby County winger, had his career cut short by injury and after six years in the Royal Army Medical Corps he qualified as a physiotherapist and also as a full FA coach. He came to Arsenal to tend to injured players when George Swindin was manager of the club and stayed to become their thirteenth manager—decidedly lucky for some! Dave Sexton was appointed chief coach in succession to Les Shannon and the pair set out to try and repair Arsenal's damaged fortunes.

Their immediate impact on Arsenal was such that the club rose to seventh in the table, thanks to an unbeaten run in their last twelve League games, and reached the fifth round of the FA Cup. In addition Mee brought several new players to the club. In September he signed inside-forward Colin Addison from Nottingham Forest. Somerset-born Addison entered League soccer with York City and joined Forest in January 1961. In his first season at Arsenal, Addison played seventeen League games.

In October, Mee brought two more players to Arsenal—players whose names would be so familiar in the Gunners' teams over the next few seasons. Bob McNab, Huddersfield Town's left-back, signed from his home town club for £50,000 after Arsenal had fought off Liverpool for his signature; and centre-forward George Graham came for a big fee with Tommy Baldwin going to Stamford Bridge in part-exchange. Previously with Aston Villa, Graham was already a Scottish under-23 international when he arrived at Highbury and he would go on to win full caps for his country. Cardiff's George Johnston was signed in March 1967, although he did not make his League debut that season; but two players who did have their first League games for Arsenal in 1966-7 were half-back John Woodward and right-winger Tommy Coakley, both Scotsmen. Don Howe was not so lucky. After breaking his leg the previous season, Howe played only once for Arsenal's First Division side in 1966-7 and was put in charge of the reserves for whom he played thirty-two games.

As Arsenal went up the table Jim Furnell and Jon Sammels played in every League match while George Armstrong and Frank McLintock missed only two games each. New signing George Graham finished leading scorer with eleven goals from his thirty-three League matches, and Peter Storey maintained his progress with thirty-four games. One of the most pleasing aspects of the season was the improvement of Peter Simpson. Simpson's total of League games before the start of the campaign was seventeen. In 1966-7 he played another thirty-four, thanks mainly to Bertie Mee who gave the youngster a new belief in himself.

Arsenal played in the Football League Cup for the first time, making hard work of beating lowly Gillingham who took the Gunners to three matches before class finally told and goals from Baldwin (two), McLintock (two) and Coakley saw

Arsenal 1966-7. Back row, left to right: Graham, Addison, McLintock, Furnell, Storey, Simpson, McNab. Front row: Neilson, Armstrong, Neill, Ure, Sammels.

the Kent side off by 5-0. Arsenal's first season in the trophy soon came to an end in the next round when West Ham beat them 3-1 at Highbury, Bristol-born David Jenkins—who was still waiting for his First Division debut—scoring Arsenal's consolation goal. In the FA Cup Arsenal's reward for beating Birmingham City would have been a plum quarter-final tie against Spurs. But it was the Blues who went through by the only goal of the game.

Football League Cup

Rnd 2	Gillingham	(h)	1-1
Replay	Gillingham	(a)	1-1
Replay	Gillingham	(h)	5-0
Rnd 3	West Ham	(h)	1-3

First Division results 1966-7

	H	A
Aston Villa	1-0	1-0
Blackpool	1-1	3-0
Burnley	0-0	4-1
Chelsea	2-1	1-3
Everton	3-1	0-0
Fulham	1-0	0-0
Leeds	0-1	1-3
Leicester	2-4	1-2
Liverpool	1-1	0-0
Manchester City	1-0	1-1
Manchester United	1-1	0-1
Newcastle	2-0	1-2
Nottingham Forest	1-1	1-2
Sheffield United	2-0	1-1
Sheffield Wednesday	1-1	1-1
Southampton	4-1	1-2
Stoke	3-1	2-2
Sunderland	2-0	3-1
Tottenham	0-2	1-3
West Brom	2-3	1-0
West Ham	2-1	2-2

Final League Record

P	W	D	L	F	A	Pts	Pos
42	16	14	12	58	47	46	7th

FA Cup

Rnd 3	Bristol Rovers	(a)	3-0
Rnd 4	Bolton	(a)	0-0
Replay	Bolton	(h)	3-0
Rnd 5	Birmingham	(a)	0-1

John Radford (No 8) fails to get the ball past Ogley and Pardoe of Manchester City at Highbury in January 1967. Arsenal won 1-0.

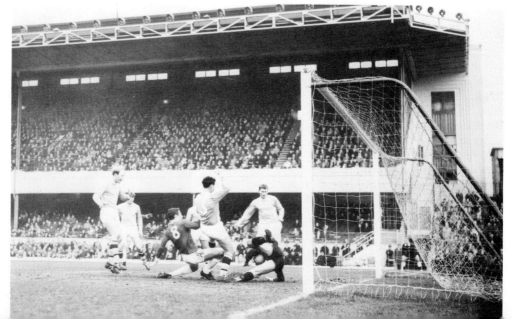

1967-8

Arsenal went to Wembley for the first time in sixteen seasons when they won through to the final of the Football League Cup against Leeds United. But the final itself was a dour affair, settled by a single goal of dubious parentage. In the First Division Arsenal finished ninth, and the FA Cup saw the Gunners again win through to the fifth round before losing the chance of a quarter-final place for the first time since 1956-7 when they again lost to Birmingham City, this time after a drawn match at Highbury.

In October 1967 Arsenal lost their coach Dave Sexton who answered the call to return to Chelsea who were struggling following a 7-0 thrashing at Leeds and the departure of Tommy Docherty. Sexton was replaced at Arsenal by Don Howe.

In the First Division Arsenal's leading scorer was again George Graham who netted sixteen goals in thirty-eight appearances. George Armstrong was the only ever-present and youngsters who made their debut were Pat Rice and George Johnston. Arsenal's big signing of the season was Bobby Gould, who signed from Coventry City in February 1968 for £99,000. Gould could not play in the Football League Cup but he made three appearances in the FA Cup, scoring the goal which gave the Gunners a 1-0 fourth round win at Swansea Town just a couple of weeks after he joined Arsenal. Gould scored again in the replay at St Andrew's but he could not prevent Birmingham City marching through to their second successive quarter-final at the expense of the Gunners.

Arsenal's Football League Cup run had started in September with a 2-1 win over Coventry City at Highfield Road, Sammels and Graham scoring Arsenal's all-important goals. The next round, the third, saw Simpson's goal beat Reading at Highbury; then Graham and Addison were on target as Blackburn Rovers went down 2-1, also at Highbury. Arsenal were now in the quarter-finals where they fought out an exciting 3-3 draw with Burnley before the Lancashire club were beaten 2-1 in the Highbury replay through Radford and Neill. The Gunners' semi-final was a two-legged affair against Huddersfield Town. In the first leg at Arsenal, Graham, Radford and McNab eased the Gunners home 3-2. The one-goal lead was suf-

ficient. At Leeds Road, Sammels, Jenkins and McLintock gave Arsenal a 6-3 aggregate win and the right to meet Leeds in the final at Wembley.

Arsenal's team that day—2 March 1968—was: Furnell, Storey, McNab, McLintock, Simpson, Ure, Radford, Jenkins, Graham, Sammels, Armstrong. Sub: Neill. Leeds won the game 1-0, thanks to a goal scored by Terry Cooper when Jim Furnell claimed that he was pushed off-balance by a Leeds attacker. Certainly the Arsenal goalkeeper suffered for most of the afternoon with big Jack Charlton forever in his way at set-pieces. But Harwich referee Mr L. J. Hamer saw nothing wrong and the goal stood. It was a shabby affair and Arsenal deserved better. They were to have a second chance the following season—a chance which was to meet with even more disasterous results.

Football League Cup

Rnd 2	Coventry	(a)	2-1
Rnd 3	Reading	(h)	1-0
Rnd 4	Blackburn	(h)	2-1
Rnd 5	Burnley	(a)	3-3
Replay	Burnley	(h)	2-1
SF 1st leg	Huddersfield	(h)	3-2
SF 2nd leg	Huddersfield	(a)	3-1
Final	Leeds	(W)	0-1

Sammels and Bremner in a mid-air dual during the Football League Cup final against Leeds at Wembley, March 1968.

Sprake, Leeds' goalkeeper, tries to clear with his feet as Graham takes the ball through the Leeds defence at Wembley.

First Division results 1967-8

	H	A
Burnley	2-0	0-1
Chelsea	1-1	1-2
Coventry	1-1	1-1
Everton	2-2	0-2
Fulham	5-3	3-1
Leeds	4-3	1-3
Leicester	2-1	2-2
Liverpool	2-0	0-2
Manchester City	1-0	1-1
Manchester United	0-2	0-1
Newcastle	0-0	1-2
Nottingham Forest	3-0	0-2
Sheffield United	1-1	4-2
Sheffield Wednesday	3-2	2-1
Southampton	0-3	0-2
Stoke	2-0	1-0
Sunderland	2-1	0-2
Tottenham	4-0	0-1
West Brom	2-1	3-1
West Ham	0-0	1-1
Wolves	0-2	2-3

Final League Record

P	W	D	L	F	A	Pts	Pos
42	17	10	15	60	56	44	9th

FA Cup

Rnd 3	Shrewsbury	(a)	1-1
Replay	Shrewsbury	(h)	2-0
Rnd 4	Swansea	(a)	1-0
Rnd 5	Birmingham	(h)	1-1
Replay	Birmingham	(a)	1-2

1968-9

Although Arsenal returned to Wembley for the second successive year they were humiliated by Third Division Swindon Town who took the Football League Cup with a fine 3-1 extra-time win over a Gunners team which, on paper at least, should have played the Wiltshire minnows off the park. Arsenal's League position improved to the point where they finished in fourth place—their highest spot for ten seasons—and for the third season in succession they reached the fifth round of the FA Cup before falling to a West Midlands side again, this time West Bromwich Albion. Six of the Arsenal side of 1968-9—Peter Storey, Peter Simpson, David Court, George Armstrong, Jon Sammels and John Radford—had played together in the youth side five seasons earlier. In addition, players like Bob Wilson had cost the club nothing. The season's two big signings were Scottish international winger Jimmy Robertson, who came from Tottenham in exchange for David Jenkins, and Northampton Town's big centre-half, John Roberts, who was transferred from the Cobblers in April for £25,000 plus another sum after a certain number of first team games.

Joy for giantkillers Swindon — despair for Arsenal. Roger Smart puts the Wiltshire side ahead in the 1969 Football League Cup final.

Arsenal started the season well—seven wins and two draws in the first nine games—and enjoyed a remarkable twelve-match period between 26 October and 11 January when they conceded only two goals. The League Cup semi-finals against Spurs were also played in this period and on 20 November over 55,000 saw John Radford's late goal decide the first leg at Highbury and Arsenal took a slim 1-0 lead to White Hart Lane for the return on 4 December. This time nearly 56,000 watched as Jimmy Greaves levelled the scores on aggregate after nearly seventy minutes but with the minutes ticking away George Armstrong floated over a corner and there was Radford again to head home the winner. It was a bad-tempered match and several arrests were made in the huge crowd to mar an otherwise great night for the Gunners.

The week before the League Cup Final Arsenal had to postpone their First Division game with Liverpool when most of the first team went down with a virus infection. With that kind of bug still lurking in their bodies, the last thing the players wanted was a heavy pitch to sap their energies still further. But this season was not one of Wembley's better years. The International Horse Show had ruined the pitch and three days before the final, England played France and turned it into a bog. Thousands of gallons of water were pumped off leaving an ankle-deep mixture of mud and sand. It was a pitch which suited Third Division Swindon—albeit a talented side which was to win promotion that season—more than First Division Arsenal. To their credit the Gunners tried to play football—but it was just not possible.

Swindon took the lead after thirty-six minutes when Ure's intended back-pass to Wilson only presented Roger Smart with a great scoring chance which he gratefully accepted. Either side of the goal Arsenal had put Swindon under pressure, only to see their goalkeeper Peter Downsborough make a string of daring and brilliant saves. Yet with only four minutes left, it was Downsborough who gave Arsenal the equaliser, racing from his goal so that Gould had only to poke the ball into an empty net. In extra-time Swindon took command—Arsenal had played themselves out. Just before the end of the first period of extra-time, cock-a-hoop Swindon went ahead again when Don Rogers scored a brilliant goal under pressure. In the dying seconds of the last period it was Rogers again who tore from the half-way line

Swindon's goalkeeper Desborough played brilliantly as Arsenal tried to get back in the game.

before rounding Wilson to make it 3-1. For Bertie Mee and Don Howe there was only one way to go now.

> *Arsenal's team for the 1969 Football League Cup final was: Wilson, Storey, McNab, McLintock, Ure, Simpson (sub Graham), Radford, Sammels, Court, Gould, Armstrong.*

First Division results 1968-9

	H	A
Burnley	2-0	1-0
Chelsea	0-1	1-2
Coventry	2-1	1-0
Everton	3-1	0-1
Ipswich	0-2	2-1
Leeds	1-2	0-2
Leicester	3-0	0-0
Liverpool	1-1	1-1
Manchester City	4-1	1-1
Manchester United	3-0	0-0
Newcastle	0-0	1-2
Nottingham Forest	1-1	2-0
QPR	2-1	1-0
Sheffield Wednesday	2-0	5-0
Southampton	0-0	2-1
Stoke	1-0	3-1
Sunderland	0-0	0-0
Tottenham	1-0	2-1
West Brom	2-0	0-1
West Ham	0-0	2-1
Wolves	3-1	0-0

Football League Cup

Rnd 2	Sunderland	(h)	1-0
Rnd 3	Scunthorpe	(a)	6-1
Rnd 4	Liverpool	(h)	2-1
Rnd 5	Blackpool	(h)	5-1
SF 1st leg	Tottenham	(h)	1-0
SF 2nd leg	Tottenham	(a)	1-1
Final	Swindon	(W)	1-3
			(aet)

Final League Record

P	W	D	L	F	A	Pts	Pos
42	22	12	8	56	27	56	4th

FA Cup

Rnd 3	Cardiff	(a)	0-0
Replay	Cardiff	(h)	2-0
Rnd 4	Charlton	(h)	2-0
Rnd 5	West Brom	(a)	0-1

aet = after extra time
(W) = Wembley

Extra-time and Don Rogers cracks home Swindon's second goal. Arsenal are down and almost out.

1969-70

Arsenal ended seventeen years without winning a major trophy by taking the Fairs Cup in an exciting two-legged final. Yet one football publication commented at the end of the season 'The present-day Arsenal side compares badly by comparison to that great combination, formed by Herbert Chapman, and nurtured by George Allison.' Only twelve months later Arsenal were to achieve what even Chapman, Allison and Whittaker could not pull off—the 'Double' of First Division Championship and FA Cup. Indeed, Arsenal's success story of the 1970s really began after that Football League Cup Final defeat of 1969. Bertie Mee said 'It all began here. A strong bond developed and we were determined that with our playing staff and organisation we were worthy of success. We decided that we would go forward—that we would not slide back.'

Yet success did not come in any of the domestic competitions. In the First Division Leeds and Everton soon forged ahead with Everton finally taking the title after a great fight by the Elland Road club around Christmas. In the League Cup Arsenal played four matches yet only reached the third round. Replays against Southampton and Everton added to the total but Kendall's goal at Goodison before 41,140 fans settled the issue in the Merseysiders' favour.

In the FA Cup Arsenal's run was even shorter when Blackpool, soon to be promoted to the First Division, knocked them out 3-2 in a replay at Bloomfield Road. This left only the Fairs Cup open to Arsenal. The Gunners were in Europe for the first time in six years and in earlier rounds they had made heavy weather of some of their ties, failing to score an away goal in the first three rounds. In the first round they beat Glentoran at home through Graham (two), and Gould, before losing 1-0 to a Henderson penalty in Northern Ireland. Then a goalless draw in Lisbon was good enough and in the return leg Graham again scored twice and Radford one as Arsenal went through 3-0 on aggregate. FC Rouen were also held to a 0-0 draw in France before Sammels's goal clinched the tie at Highbury. For the quarter-final against the Rumanian team, Dinamo Bacau, Arsenal started a European tie with both nineteen-year-olds, Charlie George and Eddie Kelly in the side for the first time. George had played against Glentoran in the away leg, and in the home leg against Rouen; Kelly had come on as substitute against Glentoran at Highbury, and in Rouen. Now both lined up

together for the start of a European match. They added flair and bite to the Gunners attack and midfield. In Rumania Sammels and Radford scored and at Highbury it was Radford (two), George (two), Sammels (two) and Graham who earned Arsenal a massive 9-1 aggregate.

The semi-final pitted Arsenal against Ajax, European Cup finalists the previous year. Two goals from George (one from the penalty spot) and one from Sammels opened up a 3-0 lead. In Amsterdam Ajax could only manage to pull one goal back through Muhren. They met the Belgian side, Anderlecht and in the first leg in Brussels found themselves 3-0 down when Devrindt and Mulder (two) hit them. And there, Arsenal's challenge might have ended, but for a substitution by Bertie Mee who pulled off George and sent on Ray Kennedy. The youngster who had been discarded by Port Vale made his debut for Arsenal in 1969-70 but played in only two League matches, plus two as a substitute. Now, before almost 40,000 fans in the seething atmosphere of a European Cup Final, he scored Arsenal's most important goal of the season.

Kennedy's goal was enough to give the Gunners a real chance at Highbury six days later. A crowd of 51,612 saw Kelly reduce the aggregate and then Radford bring the scores level. Finally Sammels

European Fairs Cup action and George Graham has just scored Arsenal's third goal in the home leg against Sporting Lisbon.

put them ahead for the first time in the tie. The scenes at the end were the greatest at Highbury for years. The players tried to do a lap of honour but the crowd prevented it, so great was their enthusiasm, although Bob Wilson did manage to get round ('I was determined to do it', he said later). Arsenal were on the threshold of a great achievement. Sadly, some players would not be around to see it. During 1969-70 Neill moved to Hull, Ure to Manchester United, Robertson to Ipswich, Court to Luton and Gould to Wolves.

> *Arsenal's team for the two-legged Fairs Cup final in 1970 was: Wilson, Storey, McNab, Kelly, McLintock, Simpson, Armstrong, Sammels, Radford, George, Graham. Kennedy substituted for George in the first leg in Brussels.*

First Division results 1969-70

	H	A
Burnley	3-2	1-0
Chelsea	0-3	0-3
Coventry	0-1	0-2
Crystal Palace	2-0	5-1
Derby	4-0	2-3
Everton	0-1	2-2
Ipswich	0-0	1-2
Leeds	1-1	0-0
Liverpool	2-1	1-0
Manchester City	1-1	1-1
Manchester United	2-2	1-2
Newcastle	0-0	1-3
Nottingham Forest	2-1	1-1
Sheffield Wednesday	0-0	1-1
Southampton	2-2	2-0
Stoke	0-0	0-0
Sunderland	3-1	1-1
Tottenham	2-3	0-1
West Brom	1-1	1-0
West Ham	2-1	1-1
Wolves	2-2	0-2

Final League Record

P	W	D	L	F	A	Pts	Pos
42	12	18	12	51	49	42	12th

FA Cup

Rnd 3	Blackpool	(h)	1-1
Replay	Blackpool	(a)	2-3

Football League Cup

Rnd 2	Southampton	(a)	1-1
Replay	Southampton	(h)	2-0
Rnd 3	Everton	(h)	0-0
Replay	Everton	(a)	0-1

Fairs Cup

Rnd 1, 1st leg	Glentoran . . . . (h)	3-0
Rnd 1, 2nd leg	Glentoran . . . . (a)	0-1
Rnd 2, 1st leg	Sporting Lisbon . . . . . (a)	0-0
Rnd 2, 2nd leg	Sporting Lisbon . . . . . (h)	3-0
Rnd 3, 1st leg	FC Rouen . . . . (a)	0-0
Rnd 3, 2nd leg	FC Rouen . . . . (h)	1-0
Rnd 4, 1st leg	Dinamo Bacau . . . . . . (a)	2-0
Rnd 4, 2nd leg	Dinamo Bacau . . . . . . (h)	7-1
SF 1st leg	Ajax . . . . (h)	3-0
SF 2nd leg	Ajax . . . . (a)	0-1
Final 1st leg	Anderlecht . . . . (a)	1-3
Final 2nd leg	Anderlecht . . . . (h)	3-0

Arsenal's first trophy for seventeen years. A mud-spattered John Radford heads the Gunners' second goal in the Fairs Cup second leg against Anderlecht.

1970-1

Arsenal win the 'Double'! At times it seemed unlikely that the Gunners would become only the second side this century to take both the League Championship and the FA Cup. In the end they won the First Division one point ahead of Leeds and the FA Cup against Liverpool in extra-time after coming from behind. The side was settled throughout and only three of the regular team—McNab, McLintock and Graham—had cost a fee. Peter Marinello, who signed for an Arsenal record of £100,000 from Hibs in January 1970, could manage only one game plus one appearance as a substitute—and after the third game of the season the lad hailed as a second George Best did not play at all.

Leeds had shot to the top of the First Division and a shattering 5-0 defeat at Stoke at the end of September suggested that Arsenal would not be one of the challengers. But there followed a run of fourteen League games without defeat—including eleven wins—and Arsenal reached the New Year

Double Winners! Frank McLintock and Charlie George hug each other after Arsenal had beaten Spurs 1-0 to take the First Division title and the first leg of the Double.

as the only club with a hope of catching Leeds. Yet even their most ardent fan could have given them little chance. On 27 March they were still six points behind Leeds with two games in hand and eight to play. Moreover, they were also 2-0 down to Stoke in the FA Cup semi-final at Hillsborough. Arsenal pulled a goal back through Storey and then in injury time they won a penalty. Peter Storey was in eyeball-to-eyeball confrontation with the world's number one goalkeeper, Gordon Banks. The atmosphere was electric but Storey kept his cool and Arsenal were level, winning the replay at Villa Park.

Arsenal began to shorten the gap in the League, helped by Leeds's defeat at home to West Brom by a bitterly disputed goal. With two weeks left Arsenal went to Leeds and seemed to have won a point until Jack Charlton scored a controversial goal. Three games left—Stoke (home), Spurs (away) and Liverpool in the FA Cup Final—three wins and the 'Double' was Arsenal's. Kelly's goal beat Stoke and then Arsenal learned that Leeds had beaten Forest. Goal average could decide it if Arsenal drew at Spurs in the last game. Arsenal went to White Hart Lane where nearly 52,000 fans saw Kennedy's late header beat Jennings. There was now only Liverpool between the Gunners and the 'Double'.

After ninety minutes of the 1971 FA Cup Final there was no score and the game went into extra-time. In the first few minutes of the first period Heighway took Thompson's pass and came forward until Arsenal's defence worked him wide. A snap shot from the narrowest of angles caught Wilson off-guard and Liverpool were 1-0 ahead, thanks to a great opportunist goal. Hall might have made it 2-0 but for Wilson's fine save, and then Arsenal were back in the game. Eddie Kelly, substituting for Storey, took the ball from Smith and Hughes and rolled it home with Graham following it over the line. Then came the winner. George was pushed up front from midfield in place of Graham. Immediately, Radford returned a pass to him and George's tremendous shot from outside the area flew into Clemence's net. Arsenal had done it.

There were those who said Arsenal lacked 'flair' in winning the League and the FA Cup, and in reaching the quarter-finals of the Fairs Cup. That was rubbish. They had done it and done it well. Herbert Chapman must have smiled down with pride.

First Division results 1970-1

Aug 15   Everton ....   (a)   2-2
(George, Graham; 49,684)

Aug 17   West Ham ....   (a)   0-0
(39,903)

Aug 22   Manchester United ......   (h)   4-0
(Radford 3, Graham; 54,117)

Aug 25   Huddersfield ....   (h)   1-0
(Kennedy; 34,848)

Aug 29   Chelsea...............   (a)   1-2
(Kelly; 53,722)

Sep 1   Leeds ....   (h)   0-0
(47,749)

Sep 5   Tottenham ....   (h)   2-0
(Armstrong 2; 48,713)

Sep 12   Burnley..............   (a)   2-1
(Radford, Kennedy; 12,675)

Sep 19   West Brom ....   (h)   6-2
(Graham 2, Kennedy 2, Armstrong, Cantello og; 33,326)

Sep 26   Stoke ....   (a)   0-5
(18,153)

Oct 3   Nottingham Forest ......   (h)   4-0
(Kennedy 3, Armstrong; 32,053)

Oct 10   Newcastle.............   (a)   1-1
(Graham; 38,000)

Oct 17   Everton ....   (h)   4-0
(Kennedy 2, Storey pen, Kelly; 50,012)

Oct 24   Coventry ....   (a)   3-1
(Radford, Graham, Kennedy; 30,007)

Oct 31   Derby ....   (h)   2-0
(Kelly, Radford; 43,023)

Nov 7   Blackpool.............   (a)   1-0
(Radford; 17,115)

Nov 14   Crystal Palace ....   (h)   1-1
(Radford; 34,503)

Nov 21   Ipswich...............   (a)   1-0
(Armstrong; 22,856)

Nov 28   Liverpool ....   (h)   2-0
(Radford, Graham; 45,097)

Dec 5   Manchester City ....   (a)   2-0
(Armstrong, Radford; 33,027)

Dec 12   Wolves ....   (h)   2-1
(Radford, Graham; 38,816)

Dec 20   Manchester United ......   (a)   3-1
(McLintock, Graham, Kennedy; 33,182)

Dec 27   Southampton..........   (h)   0-0
(34,169)

Jan 9   West Ham ....   (h)   2-0
(Graham, Kennedy; 49,007)

Jan 16   Huddersfield ....   (a)   1-2
(Kennedy; 30,455)

Jan 30   Liverpool ....   (a)   0-2
(43,847)

Feb 6   Manchester City ....   (h)   1-0
(Radford; 46,122)

Feb 20   Ipswich.................   (h)   3-2
(McLintock, Radford, George; 39,822)

Feb 27   Derby ....   (a)   0-2
(35,875)

Mar 2   Wolves ....   (a)   3-0
(Radford, Armstrong, Kennedy; 33,644)

Mar 13   Crystal Palace ....   (a)   2-0
(Graham, Sammels; 35,027)

Mar 20   Blackpool.............   (h)   1-0
(Storey; 37,372)

Apr 3   Chelsea...............   (h)   2-0
(Kennedy 2; 62,037)

Apr 6   Coventry ....   (h)   1-0
(Kennedy; 37,029)

Apr 10   Southampton...........   (a)   2-1
(Radford, McLintock; 30,231)

Apr 13   Nottingham Forest ......   (a)   3-0
(Kennedy, McLintock, George; 40,727)

Apr 17   Newcastle.............   (h)   1-0
(George; 48,106)

Apr 20   Burnley..............   (h)   1-0
(George pen; 47,484)

Apr 24   West Brom ....   (a)   2-2
(McLintock, Hartford og; 36,858)

Apr 26   Leeds ....   (a)   0-1
(48,350)

May 1   Stoke ....   (h)   1-0
(Kelly; 55,011)

May 3   Tottenham ....   (a)   1-0
(Kennedy; 51,992)

Final League Record

P	W	D	L	F	A	Pts	Pos
42	29	7	6	71	29	65	1st

Football League Goalscorers: Kennedy 19, Radford 15, Graham 11, Armstrong 7, George 5, McLintock 5, Kelly 4, Storey 2, own goals 2, Sammels 1

Football League Cup

Sep 8   (Rnd 2)   Ipswich ....   (a)   0-0
(21,564)

Sep 28   (replay)   Ipswich ....   (h)   4-0
(Roberts, Radford, Kennedy 2; 26,542)

Oct 6   (Rnd 3)   Luton.........   (a)   1-0
(Graham; 27,023)

Oct 27   (Rnd 4)   Crystal Palace   (a)   0-0
(40,451)

Nov 9   (replay)   Crystal Palace   (h)   0-2
(45,026)

Football League Cup Goalscorers: Kennedy 2, Graham 1, Radford 1, Roberts 1

FA Cup

Jan 6   (Rnd 3)   Yeovil . . . .   (a)   3-0
(Radford 2, Kennedy; 14,500)

Jan 23   (Rnd 4)   Portsmouth. . . .   (a)   1-1
(Storey pen; 39,659)

Feb 1   (replay) Portsmouth . . .   (h)   3-2
(George, Simpson, Storey pen; 47,865

Feb 17   (Rnd 5)   Man City . . . . . .   (a)   2-1
(George 2; 45,105)

Mar 6   (Rnd 6)   Leicester . . . . . .   (a)   0-0
(42,000)

Mar 15   (replay) Leicester . . . . . .   (h)   1-0
(George: 57,443)

Mar 27   SF   Stoke City . . . .   (H)   2-2
(Storey 2, 1 pen; 55,000)

Mar 31   (replay) Stoke City . . . . .   (V)   2-0
(Kennedy, Graham; 62,500)

May 8   (Final)   Liverpool . . . . . .   (W)   2-1
(Kelly, George; 100,000. After extra time)

FA Cup Goalscorers: George 5, Storey 4, Radford 2. Kennedy 2, Graham 1, Kelly 1, Simpson 1.

(W) = Wembley
(V) = Villa Park
(H) = Hillsborough

> *Arsenal's FA Cup-winning side in 1971 was: Wilson, Rice, McNab, Storey (sub Kelly), McLintock, Simpson, Armstrong, Graham, Radford, Kennedy, George.*

Frank McLintock, three times a Wembley loser, at last sees his dream come true as Arsenal complete the historic Double.

George Graham makes it 1-1 in the FA Cup final against Liverpool.

A flying header by George Armstrong nets Arsenal's second goal during their Fairs Cup match against Lazio at Highbury.

> *Jon Sammels joined Leicester for £100,000 in July 1971 after 212 league appearances (plus three as substitute) for the Gunners.*

Fairs Cup

Sep 16   (Rnd 1, 1st leg) Lazio. . .   (a)   2-2
(Radford 2; 60,000)

Sep 23   (Rnd 1, 2nd leg) Lazio . . .   (h)   2-0
(Radford, Armstrong; 53,013)

Oct 21   (Rnd 2, 1st leg) Sturm
              Graz . . . .   (a)   0-1
(18,000)

Nov 4   (Rnd 2, 2nd leg) Sturm
              Graz . . . .   (h)   2-0
(Kennedy, Storey pen; 37,677)

Dec 2   (Rnd 3, 1st leg) Beveren   (h)   4-0
(Graham, Kennedy 2, Sammels; 33,444)

Dec 16   (Rnd 3, 2nd leg) Beveren   (a)   0-0
(14,000)

Mar 9   (QF, 1st leg) Cologne . . .   (h)   2-1
(McLintock, Storey; 40,007)

Mar 23   (QF 2nd leg) Cologne . . .   (a)   0-1
(40,000) Arsenal lost on aggregate, away goals counting double.

Fairs Cup Goalscorers: Kennedy 3, Radford 3, Storey 2, Graham 1, Armstrong 1, Sammels 1, McLintock 1.

1971-2

After their achievements of the previous season Arsenal could only win the European Cup to improve on their epic performances. But it was not to be and the Gunners ended the 1971-2 campaign without a major trophy on show, although they did have the honour of appearing in the FA Cup Final which celebrated 100 years of the world's most famous knockout club competition.

In the First Division the Gunners ended the season in fifth place, six points behind the champions, Derby County, who they helped to the title by holding Liverpool 0-0 at Highbury in the last match. In the League Cup there was a fourth round replay defeat at the hands of Sheffield United. but the European Cup trail had got off to an e start with matches against Stromgodset and Grasshoppers, who were beaten 5-0 on aggregate. The quarter-final brought Arsenal up against the 'Flying Dutchmen' of Ajax. This time the Dutch masters were not going to be beaten by Arsenal. In Amsterdam Arsenal took a fifteenth minute lead when Ray Kennedy stunned a 65,000 crowd by capitalising on a defensive mistake. Keizer tried a back-header to Stuy and the Arsenal player jabbed a toe at the ball and sent it into the net. But it was against the run of play and fifteen minutes later the Dutchmen were level when Simpson got in the way of Muhren's twenty-yarder and diverted it past Wilson. Fifteen minutes from the end Muhren scored again from the spot.

Yet, even though Ajax had hit the woodwork twice and Wilson had pulled off a string of brave saves, Arsenal must have fancied their chances with an away goal under their belts. Ajax thought differently and after fourteen minutes of the second leg they increased their lead. Krol swung over a hopeful cross and George Graham headed it to where he thought Wilson was positioned. The ball went one way, Wilson went the other, and the game was effectively over. Without the suspended Radford, Arsenal's tactic of pumping high balls into the Dutch penalty area was ineffective. Twice more Ajax might have scored when Keizer muffed chances laid on by Cruyff. Four goals had been scored in the tie—all of dubious pedigree—and Arsenal were out of Europe.

The semi-final of the FA Cup brought a repeat performance against Stoke, this time a 1-1 draw at Villa Park when Simpson put through his own goal. Seventeen minutes from the end, Bob Wilson was carried off with cartilage trouble, John Radford taking over in goal, and in the replay Geoff Barnett helped Arsenal through 2-1. The final against Leeds was settled when Allan Clarke scored after fifty-three minutes. Alan Ball, signed for an Arsenal record of £220,000 from Everton just before Christmas, left Wembley empty-handed. Arsenal had failed to recapture the great days of just twelve months earlier.

Ray Kennedy opens the scoring in the European Cup match against Stromgodset.

First Division results 1971-2

Aug 14   Chelsea ....   (h)   3-0
(McLintock, Kennedy, Radford; 49,174)

Aug 17   Huddersfield ....   (a)   1-0
(Kennedy; 21,279)

Aug 20   Manchester United ......   (a)   1-3
(McLintock; 27,649)

Aug 24   Sheffield United ....   (h)   0-1
(45,399)

Aug 28   Stoke ....   (h)   0-1
(37,637)

Sep 4   West Brom ....   (a)   1-0
(Roberts; 29,992)

Sep 11   Leeds ....   (h)   2-0
(Graham, Storey pen; 51,196)

Sep 18   Everton ....   (a)   1-2
(Kennedy; 39,710)

Sep 25   Leicester ....   (h)   3-0
(Radford 2, Rice; 40,201)

Oct 2   Southampton ....   (a)   1-0
(Simpson; 23,738)

Oct 9   Newcastle ....   (h)   4-2
(Graham, Kelly, Kennedy, Armstrong; 40,509)

Oct 16   Chelsea ....   (a)   2-1
(Kennedy 2; 52,338)

Oct 23   Derby ....   (a)   1-2
(Graham; 36,480)

Oct 30   Ipswich ....   (h)   2-1
(Sivell og, George; 39,065)

Nov 6   Liverpool ....   (a)   2-3
(Kennedy, Smith og; 46,929)

Nov 13   Manchester City ....   (h)   1-2
(Nelson; 47,443)

Nov 20   Wolves ....   (a)   1-5
(Kennedy; 28,831)

Nov 24   Tottenham ....   (a)   1-1
(Kennedy); 52,884)

Nov 27   Crystal Palace ....   (h)   2-1
(Kelly, Radford; 32,461)

Dec 4   West Ham ....   (a)   0-0
(35,155)

Dec 11   Coventry ....   (h)   2-0
(Radford 2; 28,599)

Dec 18   West Brom ....   (h)   2-0
(Roberts 2; 28,177)

Dec 27   Nottingham Forest ......   (a)   1-1
(Graham; 42,750)

Jan 1   Everton ....   (h)   1-1
(Simpson; 47,031)

Jan 8   Stoke ....   (a)   0-0
(18,965)

Jan 22   Huddersfield ....   (h)   1-0
(Armstrong; 36,670)

Jan 29   Sheffield United ....   (a)   5-0
(George 2, Graham, Simpson, Kennedy; 30,778)

Feb 12   Derby ....   (h)   2-0
(George 2 (1 pen); 52,055)

Feb 19   Ipswich ....   (a)   1-0
(George; 28,657)

Mar 4   Manchester City ....   (a)   0-2
(44,213)

Mar 11   Newcastle ....   (a)   0-2
(31,920)

Mar 25   Leeds ....   (a)   0-3
(45,055)

Mar 28   Southampton ....   (h)   1-0
(Marinello; 27,172)

Apr 1   Nottingham Forest ......   (h)   3-0
(Kennedy, George pen, Graham; 33,895)

Apr 4   Leicester ....   (a)   0-0
(27,431)

Apr 8   Wolves ....   (h)   2-1
(Graham 2; 38,189)

Apr 11   Crystal Palace ....   (a)   2-2
(Radford, Ball; 34,384)

Apr 22   West Ham ....   (h)   2-1
(Ball 2; 45,251)

Apr 25   Manchester United ......   (h)   3-0
(Kennedy, Simpson, Radford; 49,125)

May 1   Coventry ....   (a)   1-0
(McLintock; 23,509)

May 8   Liverpool ....   (h)   0-0
(39,289)

May 11   Tottenham ....   (h)   0-2
(42,038)

Final League Record

P	W	D	L	F	A	Pts	Pos
42	22	8	12	58	40	52	5th

Football League Goalscorers: Kennedy 12, Radford 8, Graham 8, George 7, Simpson 4, McLintock 3, Roberts 3, Ball 3, Kelly 2, Armstrong 2, Rice 1, Nelson 1, Marinello 1, Storey 1, own goals 2.

Bertie Mee welcomes Alan Ball to Highbury after the England player signed from Everton in December 1971.

Peter Lorimer's shot hits the post as Leeds United press during the 1972 FA Cup final.

Arsenal's team which reached the 1972 FA Cup final before losing to Leeds was: Barnett, Rice, McNab, Storey, McLintock, Simpson, Armstrong, Ball, Radford (sub Kennedy), George, Graham.

FA Cup

Jan 15 (Rnd 3) Swindon ...... (a) 2-0
(Armstrong, Ball; 32,000)
Feb 5 (Rnd 4) Reading .... (a) 2-1
(Morgan og, Rice; 25,756)
Feb 26 (Rnd 5) Derby .... (a) 2-2
(George 2; 39,662)
Feb 29 (replay) Derby .... (h) 0-0
(63,077)
Mar 13 (replay) Derby .... (n) 1-0
(Kennedy ; 40,000)
Mar 18 (Rnd 6) Orient .... (a) 1-0
(Ball; 31,678)
Apr 15 (SF) Stoke City .... (n) 1-1
(Armstrong; 56,576)
Apr 19 (replay) Stoke City ..... (n) 2-1
(George pen, Radford; 38,970)
May 6 (Final) Leeds .... (W) 0-1
(100,000)

FA Cup Goalscorers: George 3, Armstrong 2, Ball 2, Kennedy 1, Radford 1, Rice 1, own goal 1.
(W) = Wembley

Football League Cup

Sep 8 (Rnd 2) Barnsley...... (h) 1-0
(Kennedy; 27,294)
Oct 6 (Rnd 3) Newcastle ..... (h) 4-0
(Radford 2, Kennedy, Graham; 34,071)
Oct 26 (Rnd 4) Sheffield United (h) 0-0
(44,061)
Nov 8 (replay) Sheffield United (a) 0-2
(35,461)

Football League Cup Goalscorers: Radford 2, Kennedy 2, Graham 1

European Cup

Sep 15 (Rnd 1, 1st leg)
Stromgodset .... (a) 3-1
(Simpson, Wolner og, Kelly; 22,000)
Sep 29 (Rnd 1, 2nd leg)
Stromgodset .... (h) 4-0
(Kennedy, Radford 2, Armstrong; 27,176)
Oct 20 (Rnd 2, 1st leg)
Grasshoppers.......... (a) 2-0
(Kennedy, Graham; 18,000)
Nov 3 (Rnd 2, 2nd leg)
Grasshoppers.......... (h) 3-0
(Kennedy, George, Radford; 31,106)
Mar 8 (QF, 1st leg) Ajax (a) 1-2
(Kennedy; 65,000)
Mar 22 (QF, 2nd leg) Ajax ..... (h) 0-1
(56,145)

European Cup Goalscorers: Kennedy 4, Radford 3, Simpson 1, Kelly 1, Armstrong 1, Graham 1, George 1, own goal 1

1972-3

Arsenal again had nothing tangible to show for their efforts in 1972-3. They finished runners-up to Leeds after starting the season in fine style, reached the semi-final of the FA Cup, and the quarter-final of the Football League Cup before missing out on both trophies. There was a bad start to the season before a ball had been kicked in real competition. In August, Arsenal lost 4-0 in a pre-season friendly in Hamburg when Pat Rice was taken off with an ankle injury. When the League season opened Charlie George was missing with a hamstring injury and John Roberts asked for a transfer after being named as substitute by Bertie Mee. Then George, recalled in place of the injured Radford, found himself in the middle of a pay dispute with Arsenal. Yet Arsenal made a fine start. They went the first seven matches without defeat and were always around the top of the table. On 16 September, during the 0-0 draw with Liverpool at Highbury, Jimmy Hill, BBC commentator and former Coventry team manager, took over from an injured linesman. And by 14 October, with the £200,000 signing of Coventry's Jeff Blockley completed, Arsenal were second in the First Division, just one point behind Liverpool. A week earlier, Alan Ball was sent off at Bramall Lane and ten-men Arsenal went down 1-0. But on 15 October there was better news for the club when Charlie George came off the transfer list.

October was certainly an eventful month for Arsenal. Unsettled John Roberts signed for Birmingham to give Arsenal a record incoming fee of £140,000; and Peter Marinello was named in the Scotland squad to play Denmark; Bob Wilson was named for the same match although he had still to play a League match for Arsenal after his comeback from injury in the previous season's FA Cup semi-final.

> *Tommy Docherty signed George Graham for Manchester United in December 1972 for £120,000. 'He's like Gunter Netzer!' said the Doc.*

Wilson's comeback was not far away—and what a match the goalkeeper chose to return to the big time. His first game back between the Arsenal posts was at Derby where the rampant Rams won 5-0. A week later Arsenal were involved in a bitter game with Leeds at Highbury. There were two

penalties (one for each side) and a Radford centre palmed into the Leeds goal by Harvey gave Arsenal both points. Referee Clive Thomas booked five Leeds players and Arsenal's Ball in a bruising game. Eddie Kelly, who had been on the transfer list, decided to stay at Highbury and he helped them through to the semi-final of the FA Cup before they lost 2-1 to Sunderland—shock winners of the trophy—at Hillsborough.

The Gunners had been second in the table since that December win over Leeds, taking over the lead for a short time in February, but it was to Anfield that the title finally went. At the end of the season Frank McLintock moved to QPR for £25,000; and Peter Marinello signed for Portsmouth, officially joining the Fratton Park club after Arsenal's summer tour. On 21 April Eddie Hapgood, a Chapman hero, died, aged sixty-four.

Football League Cup

Sep 5	(Rnd 2)	Everton	(h)	1-0
(Storey; 35,115)				
Oct 3	(Rnd 3)	Rotherham	(h)	5-0
(George, Marinello, Storey, Radford 2; 25,241)				
Oct 31	(Rnd 4)	Sheffield United	(a)	2-1
(George, Radford; 20,128)				
Nov 21	(Rnd 5)	Norwich	(h)	0-3
(37,671)				

Football League Cup Goalscorers: Radford 3, Storey 2, George 2, Marinello 1

Crystal Palace striker John Craven lets fly past Jeff Blockley and Bob McNab at Highbury, October 1972.

First Division results 1972-3

Aug 12   Leicester .... (a)   1-0
(Ball pen; 28,009)
Aug 15   Wolves .... (h)   5-2
(Radford 2, Kennedy, Simpson, McNab; 38,524)
Aug 19   Stoke .... (h)   2-0
(Kennedy 2; 42,146)
Aug 22   Coventry .... (a)   1-1
(Graham; 24,616)
Aug 26   Manchester United ...... (a)   0-0
(48,108)
Aug 29   West Ham .... (h)   1-0
(Ball pen; 43,802)
Sep 2   Chelsea .... (h)   1-1
(Webb og; 46,675)
Sep 9   Newcastle .... (a)   1-2
(Kennedy; 23,849)
Sep 16   Liverpool .... (h)   0-0
(47,597)
Sep 23   Norwich .... (a)   2-3
(Storey, Radford; 32,237)
Sep 26   Birmingham .... (h)   2-0
(Storey, George; 30,003)
Sep 30   Southampton .... (h)   1-0
(Graham; 34,694)
Oct 7   Sheffield United .... (a)   0-1
(24,478)
Oct 14   Ipswich .... (h)   1-0
(Graham; 34,196)
Oct 21   Crystal Palace .... (a)   3-2
(George pen, Radford, Rice; 35,865)
Oct 28   Manchester City .... (h)   0-0
(45,536)
Nov 4   Coventry .... (h)   0-2
(33,699)
Nov 11   Wolves .... (a)   3-1
(Radford 2, Marinello; 25,988)
Nov 18   Everton .... (h)   1-0
(Radford; 35,728)
Nov 25   Derby .... (a)   0-5
(31,034)
Dec 2   Leeds .... (h)   2-1
(Ball pen, Radford; 39,108)
Dec 9   Tottenham .... (a)   2-1
(Storey, Radford; 47,505)
Dec 16   West Brom .... (h)   2-1
(Nisbett og, Radford; 27,119)
Dec 23   Birmingham .... (a)   1-1
(Kelly; 32,721)
Dec 26   Norwich .... (h)   2-0
(Radford, Ball; 39,038)
Dec 30   Stoke .... (a)   0-0
(24,586)
Jan 6   Manchester United ...... (h)   3-1
(Kennedy, Armstrong, Ball; 56,194)
Jan 20   Chelsea .... (a)   1-0
(Kennedy; 36,292)

Jan 27   Newcastle .... (h)   2-2
(Kennedy, Ball; 37,906)
Feb 10   Liverpool .... (a)   2-0
(Ball pen, Radford; 49,898)
Feb 17   Leicester .... (h)   1-0
(Manley og; 42,047)
Feb 28   West Brom .... (a)   0-1
(23,515)
Mar 3   Sheffield United .... (h)   3-2
(George 2, Ball; 33,336)
Mar 10   Ipswich .... (a)   2-1
(Radford, Ball pen; 33,525)
Mar 24   Manchester City .... (a)   2-1
(George, Kennedy; 33,031)
Mar 26   Crystal Palace .... (h)   1-0
(Ball; 41,879)
Mar 31   Derby .... (h)   0-1
(45,217)
Apr 14   Tottenham .... (h)   1-1
(Storey; 50,863)
Apr 21   Everton .... (a)   0-0
(42,888)
Apr 23   Southampton .... (a)   2-2
(George, Radford; 23,919)
Apr 28   West Ham .... (a)   2-1
(Kennedy, Radford; 37,366)
May 9   Leeds .... (a)   1-6
(Armstrong; 25,088)

Final League Record

P	W	D	L	F	A	Pts	Pos
42	23	11	8	57	43	57	2nd

Football League Goalscorers: Radford 15, Ball 10, Kennedy 9, George 6, Storey 4, Graham 3, Armstrong 2, Rice 1, Simpson 1, McNab 1, Marinello 1, Kelly 1, own goals 3

FA Cup

Jan 13 (Rnd 3) Leicester ...... (h)   2-2
(Kennedy, Armstrong; 36,433)
Jan 17 (replay) Leicester ...... (a)   2-1
(Radford, Kelly; 33,000)
Feb 4 (Rnd 4) Bradford City .. (h)   2-0
(Ball, George; 40,407)
Feb 24 (Rnd 5) Carlisle .... (a)   2-1
(Ball, McLintock; 24,000)
Mar 17 (Rnd 6) Chelsea .... (a)   2-2
(Ball, George; 37,685)
Mar 20 (replay) Chelsea .... (h)   2-1
(Ball pen, Kennedy; 62,642)
Apr 7 (SF) Sunderland .... (n)   1-2
(George; 55,000)

FA Cup Goalscorers: Ball 4, George 3, Kennedy 2, Armstrong 1, Radford 1, Kelly 1, McLintock 1

1973-4

A 3-0 win over Manchester United at Highbury on the first day of the season no doubt lifted spirits at Arsenal Stadium. But this was not to be a season of success. Arsenal had rocketed to twentieth place in the First Division by the fifth game of the season with defeats against Leeds (at home 1-2), at Sheffield United (0-5), and at home to Leicester (0-2). The season was still young, of course, and a couple of wins in the next two matches soon had the Gunners back up the table to eleventh spot. But the damage was done and Arsenal were never in a position to man a real challenge on the First Division title which was taken by Leeds. The Gunners ended the season in tenth place, some twenty points adrift of the leading club. In the Cups it was a similar story. There was a shock 1-0 defeat at the hands of lowly Tranmere Rovers—who had the temerity to come to Highbury and inflict the damage—in the second round of the Football League Cup; and in the FA Cup, after beating Norwich 1-0, Arsenal fell 2-0 in a replay at Villa Park.

Bob Wilson was back between the posts full-time, save for one match near the end of the season when former Manchester United goalkeeper Jimmy Rimmer deputised. And there were several new faces making their first ap-

pearances with Arsenal—faces that would soon become as familiar as the famous names they sometimes replaced.

Among them was a young Irish boy called Liam Brady. Brady came on as substitute in the game against Birmingham on 6 October 1973 and made his first full League appearance the following week at White Hart Lane. He made nine appearances altogether that season, together with another four as substitute, and scored his first goal for the club in the very last game of the season when he helped Arsenal to a 1-1 draw at home to Queens Park Rangers, equalising in the second-half after Rangers had gone in 1-0 ahead at half-time. Richie Powling also made his debut, playing in just two games, and David Price played in the opening game of the season—his first full game in an Arsenal First Division shirt. Arsenal

FA Cup

Jan 5	(Rnd 3)	Norwich	(a)	1-0
(Kelly; 21,500)				
Jan 26	(Rnd 4)	Aston Villa	(h)	1-1
(Kennedy; 41,682)				
Jan 30	(replay)	Aston Villa	(a)	0-2
(47,821)				

FA Cup Goalscorers: Kelly 1, Kennedy 1

Football League Cup

Oct 2	(Rnd 2)	Tranmere	(h)	0-1
(20,337)				

Bob Wilson's superb effort fails to prevent Stan Bowles putting QPR a goal up in what was the Arsenal goalkeeper's farewell game at Highbury

also had two young apprentices on their books by this time—Frank Stapleton and David O'Leary.

But the one player who had continued to make strides was Ray Kennedy—the man who was turned down by Port Vale. Kennedy played in all forty-two League games—the only Arsenal player to do so in 1973-4—and scored twelve goals. It was to be his last season at Highbury. During the 1974 close season the League runners-up Liverpool paid Arsenal £180,000 for Kennedy. Soon he was to win new honours with the Merseysiders and can always be proud that he was Bill Shankly's last big signing. Three days after Kennedy's move to Anfield, Arsenal replaced him with Manchester United's Brian Kidd who came south for £110,000.

First Division results 1973-4

Aug 25   Manchester United ......   (h)   3-0
(Kennedy, Radford, Ball; 51,501)
Aug 28   Leeds ....   (h)   1-2
(Blockley; 47,429)
Sep 1   Newcastle............   (a)   1-1
(George; 28,697)
Sep 4   Sheffield United ....   (a)   0-5
(27,839)
Sep 8   Leicester ....   (h)   0-2
(28,558)
Sep 11   Sheffield United ....   (h)   1-0
(Kennedy; 29,434)
Sep 15   Norwich ....   (a)   4-0
(George, McNab, Ball pen, Kennedy; 29,278)
Sep 22   Stoke ....   (h)   2-1
(Radford, Ball; 30,578)
Sep 29   Everton ....   (a)   0-1
(31,359)
Oct 6   Birmingham...........   (h)   1-0
(Kennedy; 23,915)
Oct 13   Tottenham............   (a)   0-2
(41,856)
Oct 20   Ipswich ....   (h)   1-1
(Simpson; 28,344)
Oct 27   QPR ....   (a)   0-2
(29,115)
Nov 3   Liverpool ....   (h)   0-2
(39,837)
Nov 10   Manchester City ....   (a)   2-1
(Kelly, Hornsby; 34,041)
Nov 17   Chelsea...............   (h)   0-0
(38,677)
Nov 24   West Ham ....   (a)   3-1
(George, Ball 2; 28,287)
Dec 1   Coventry ....   (h)   2-2
(Hornsby, Nelson; 22,340)
Dec 4   Wolves ....   (h)   2-2
(George, McAlle og; 13,482)

Dec 8   Derby ....   (a)   1-1
(Newton og; 25,161)
Dec 15   Burnley...............   (a)   1-2
(Radford; 13,200)
Dec 22   Everton ....   (h)   1-0
(Ball; 19,896)
Dec 26   Southampton..........   (a)   1-1
(Ball; 24,153)
Dec 29   Leicester.............   (a)   0-2
(25,860)
Jan 1   Newcastle.............   (h)   0-1
(29,258)
Jan 12   Norwich ....   (h)   2-0
(Ball 2; 22,084)
Jan 19   Manchester United ......   (a)   1-1
(Kennedy; 38,589)
Feb 2   Burnley..............   (h)   1-1
(Ball; 20,789)
Feb 5   Leeds ....   (a)   1-3
(Ball; 26,778)
Feb 16   Tottenham ....   (h)   0-1
(38,804)
Feb 23   Birmingham............   (a)   1-3
(Kennedy; 29,822)
Mar 2   Southampton..........   (h)   1-0
(Ball; 19,210)
Mar 16   Ipswich...............   (a)   2-2
(Kennedy, Simpson; 22,297)
Mar 23   Manchester City ....   (h)   2-0
(Radford 2; 25,319)
Mar 30   Stoke ....   (a)   0-0
(18,532)
Apr 6   West Ham ....   (h)   0-0
(37,868)
Apr 13   Chelsea...............   (a)   3-1
(Kennedy 2, Radford; 29,152)
Apr 15   Wolves ....   (a)   1-3
(Kennedy; 25,881)
Apr 20   Derby ....   (h)   2-0
(Ball pen, George; 26,017)
Apr 24   Liverpool ....   (a)   1-0
(Kennedy; 47,997)
Apr 27   Coventry ....   (a)   3-3
(Rice, Kennedy, Radford; 19,945)
Apr 30   QPR ....   (h)   1-1
(Brady; 40,396)

Final League Record

P	W	D	L	F	A	Pts	Pos
42	14	14	14	49	51	42	10th

Football League Goalscorers: Ball 13, Kennedy 12, Radford 7, George 5, Simpson 2, Hornsby 2, Blockley 1, McNab 1, Kelly 1, Nelson 1, Rice 1, Brady 1, own goals 2

1974-5

Bob Wilson had played his last game for Arsenal in the final match of the previous season, having retired to work in television, and Arsenal took the field for the first match of 1974-5 with Jimmy Rimmer as his replacement. Wilson had played 234 League games for the Gunners. During the season Jeff Blockley moved to Leicester City—his hometown club—for £100,000, well below the figure which Arsenal had paid to Coventry for the centre-half some eighteen months earlier. New players also came to Highbury. In October veteran centre-half Terry Mancini joined Arsenal from QPR for £20,000; and in December Alex Cropley, Hibernian's Scottish international winger, came for £150,000. Londoner John Matthews made his League debut in the first match of the season and played in twenty games; and Bob McNab played his last game in an Arsenal shirt.

Before he left, McNab shared in an unfortunate piece of history for Arsenal. During the game against Derby County at the Baseball Ground on 22 February, both he and Alan Ball were sent off. The last time two players from the same club had been sent off in the same match was in 1967 when McLintock and Storey received their marching orders—an unfortunate double for the Gunners. For much of the first-half of the season Arsenal hovered in the lower half of the First Division. In October they were actually twenty-second in the table, but Kidd led the way with nineteen goals, playing in all but two League games, and slowly Arsenal went away from the danger zone.

Alan Ball puts Arsenal in the lead against Liverpool in February 1975 at Highbury.

In March 1975 a young Irish boy made his debut for Arsenal. Frank Stapleton, Dublin-born and signed as a Highbury apprentice in June 1972, played in the 1-1 draw at home to Stoke and although he was substituted in favour of Brady, he had done enough to convince the fans that they had seen a 'good 'un'. In 1980-1 Stapleton scored his one hundredth goal in top class football to repay that faith.

In the FA Cup Arsenal reached the sixth round after three energy-sapping fifth round ties with Leicester City. The sides drew 0-0 and 1-1 before Radford got the only goal of the second replay after the sides had tied yet again, 0-0 at the end of ninety minutes. The sixth round against London neighbours West Ham United on 8 March was a sad day for Gunners fans. Surprise choice Alan Taylor scored twice before nearly 57,000 fans at Highbury and Arsenal had lost their first-ever home FA Cup-tie to a London club. Arsenal ended the season empty-handed once more. It was a strange experience after the euphoria of the very early 1970s. But a new breed of Gunner was on the way up—and soon the gunfire of Highbury would be heard once more.

FA Cup

Jan 4	(Rnd 3)	York	(h)	1-1
(Kelly; 27,029)				
Jan 7	(replay)	York	(a)	3-1
(Kidd 3; 15,362)				
Jan 25	(Rnd 4)	Coventry	(a)	1-1
(Ball; 31,165)				
Jan 29	(replay)	Coventry	(h)	3-0
(Armstrong 2, Matthews; 30,827)				
Feb 15	(Rnd 5)	Leicester	(h)	0-0
(43,841)				
Feb 19	(replay)	Leicester	(a)	1-1
(Radford; 35,009)				
Feb 24	(replay)	Leicester	(a)	1-0
(Radford; 39,025)				
Mar 8	(Rnd 6)	West Ham	(h)	0-2
(56,742)				

FA Cup Goalscorers: Kidd 3, Radford 2, Armstrong 2, Kelly 1, Ball 1, Matthews 1

Football League Cup

Sep 10	(Rnd 2)	Leicester	(h)	1-1
(Kidd; 20,788)				
Sep 18	(replay)	Leicester	(a)	1-2
(Brady; 17,303)				

Football League Cup Goalscorers: Kidd 1, Brady 1

Peter Simpson and Terry Mancini fight it out with Spurs John Duncan at Highbury, April 1975.

First Division results 1974-5

Aug 17   Leicester . . . .   (a)   1-0
(Kidd; 26,448)

Aug 20   Ipswich . . . .   (h)   0-1
(31,027)

Aug 24   Manchester City . . . .   (h)   4-0
(Kidd 2, Radford 2; 27,143)

Aug 27   Ipswich . . . .   (a)   0-3
(28,035)

Aug 31   Everton . . . .   (a)   1-2
(Kidd; 42,438)

Sep 7   Burnley . . . .   (h)   0-1
(23,546)

Sep 14   Chelsea . . . .   (a)   0-0
(34,596)

Sep 21   Luton . . . .   (h)   2-2
(Kidd 2; 21,629)

Sep 28   Birmingham . . . .   (a)   1-3
(George; 25,584)

Oct 5   Leeds . . . .   (a)   0-2
(32,784)

Oct 12   QPR . . . .   (h)   2-2
(Kidd, Radford; 29,690)

Oct 16   Manchester City . . . .   (a)   1-2
(Radford; 26,658)

Oct 19   Tottenham . . . .   (a)   0-2
(36,914)

Oct 26   West Ham . . . .   (h)   3-0
(Radford, Kidd, Brady; 41,004)

Nov 2   Wolves . . . .   (h)   0-0
(27,572)

Nov 9   Liverpool . . . .   (a)   3-1
(Ball 2, Brady; 43,850)

Nov 16   Derby . . . .   (h)   3-1
(Ball 2 (1 pen), Kidd; 32,286)

Nov 23   Coventry . . . .   (a)   0-3
(15,669)

Nov 30   Middlesbrough . . . .   (h)   2-0
(Brady, Ball pen; 25,283)

Dec 7   Carlisle . . . .   (a)   1-2
(Kidd; 12,926)

Dec 14   Leicester . . . .   (h)   0-0
(20,849)

Dec 21   Stoke . . . .   (a)   2-0
(Kidd 2; 23,292)

Dec 26   Chelsea . . . .   (h)   1-2
(Ball pen; 33,784)

Dec 28   Sheffield United . . . .   (a)   1-1
(George; 19,967)

Jan 11   Carlisle . . . .   (h)   2-1
(Radford, Cropley; 21,538)

Jan 18   Middlesbrough . . . .   (a)   0-0
(27,996)

Feb 1   Liverpool . . . .   (h)   2-0
(Ball 2 (1 pen); 43,028)

Feb 8   Wolves . . . .   (a)   0-1
(19,807)

Feb 22   Derby . . . .   (a)   1-2
(Radford; 24,002)

Mar 1   Everton . . . .   (h)   0-2
(32,216)

Mar 15   Birmingham . . . .   (h)   1-1
(Kidd; 17,845)

Mar 18   Newcastle . . . .   (h)   3-0
(Kidd, Ball pen, Rostron; 16,540)

Mar 22   Burnley . . . .   (a)   3-3
(Rostron, Hornsby 2; 17,539)

Mar 25   Luton . . . .   (a)   0-2
(22,101)

Mar 29   Stoke . . . .   (h)   1-1
(Kelly; 26,852)

Mar 31   Sheffield United . . . .   (h)   1-0
(Kidd; 24,338)

Apr 8   Coventry . . . .   (h)   2-0
(Kidd 2; 17,291)

Apr 12   Leeds . . . .   (h)   1-2
(Kidd; 36,619)

Apr 19   QPR . . . .   (a)   0-0
(24,362)

Apr 23   Newcastle . . . .   (a)   1-3
(Hornsby; 21,895)

Apr 26   Tottenham . . . .   (h)   1-0
(Kidd; 43,752)

Apr 28   West Ham . . . .   (a)   0-1
(30,195)

Final League Record

P	W	D	L	F	A	Pts	Pos
42	13	11	18	47	49	37	16th

Football League Goalscorers: Kidd 19, Ball 9, Radford 7, Brady 3, Hornsby 3, George 2, Rostron 2, Kelly 1, Cropley 1

1975-6

Arsenal started the season without Charlie George. They finished it without Bertie Mee. In between Arsenal endured one of their worst seasons in recent years. They finished seventeenth in the First Division and went out of the FA Cup and the Football League Cup at the first hurdles. In July 1975 George seemed all set to join Terry Neill at Tottenham. Then Dave Mackay stepped in and whisked the player away from under the noses of his old club and up the M1 to Derby's Baseball Ground where the player was to enjoy a second taste of European Cup soccer with the new champions. George went for £90,000 and a disappointed Neill could only say, 'There's nothing to be gained by worrying about it.'

Arsenal lost a pre-season friendly at Dundee where Eddie Kelly skippered the Gunners in place of the transfer-listed Alan Ball and on the first day of the season they were held to a goalless draw at Turf Moor. In the midweek game at Bramall Lane Sammy Nelson was sent off and was automatically suspended for one match and collected twelve penalty points under the new disciplinary system, Arsenal losing 3-1. On a much sadder note, Wally Barnes, Arsenal's right-back in the years after World War II, died on 4 September, aged fifty-five. Arsenal then dipped out of the Football League Cup, losing their replayed second round tie at Everton.

On 15 November Arsenal lost 3-1 to Birmingham and slipped down to eighteenth place in the table and they stayed around that position for much of the remainder of the season. Arsenal's lone goal at St Andrew's was scored by Alan Ball and the following day the former England skipper asked to come off the transfer list. By Christmas Arsenal were still in the relegation zone and a brief respite from the worries of the League only served to see the Gunners dumped out of the FA Cup when Wolves trounced them 3-0 at Molineux. Twelve days later Eddie Kelly was placed on the transfer list and in March, with Arsenal still struggling, Peter Storey was suspended for fourteen days for allegedly not reporting for training. Storey's reaction was to vow that he would never kick a ball for the club again: 'I'm fed up with reserve team football', he said. Storey was still at Highbury the following season, but one player who did leave early in 1976 was Geoff Barnett, the man who had deputised so well when Wilson was injured two years previously.

On 20 March Arsenal beat West Ham 6-1 with the help of a Kidd hat-trick and there was enough improvement in the side's performances to lift them clear of the danger zone, although in the end their seventeenth position, while six points away from relegation, was still Arsenal's worst League placing since 1924-5. During the final weeks of the season Bertie Mee announced that he would retire once Arsenal were safe: 'The pressures on an Arsenal manager are sometimes intolerable', he said.

There was a rumour that Miljan Miljanic, the Yugoslavian team boss of European legends Real Madrid would soon be coming to Arsenal. This proved to be untrue and soon an old Arsenal favourite would be back at his old club. Three days after the last League game of the season Arsenal placed Brian Kidd and young Brian Hornsby on the transfer list along with Kelly. None of them would play for the Gunners again, Kidd signing for Manchester City for £100,000 in the close season.

Manchester City's Asa Hartford sends Jimmy Rimmer the wrong way to put his side 3-0 up at Highbury, October 1975.

FA Cup
Jan 3   (Rnd 3)   Wolves . . . .   (a)   0-3
(22,215)

Football League Cup
Sep 9   (Rnd 2)   Everton . . . . . .   (a)   2-2
(Cropley, Stapleton; 17,174)
Sep 23   (replay)   Everton . . . . . .   (h)   0-1
(21,813)
Football League Cup Goalscorers: Cropley 1, Stapleton 1

First Division results 1975-6

Aug 16   Burnley .... (a)   0-0
(18,603)

Aug 19   Sheffield United .... (a)   3-1
(Brady, Rice, Kidd; 23,344)

Aug 23   Stoke .... (h)   0-1
(28,025)

Aug 26   Norwich .... (h)   2-1
(Ball pen, Kidd; 22,613)

Aug 30   Wolves .... (a)   0-0
(18,144)

Sep 6   Leicester .... (h)   1-1
(Stapleton; 22,005)

Sep 13   Aston Villa .... (a)   0-2
(34,474)

Sep 20   Everton .... (h)   2-2
(Kidd, Stapleton; 24,864)

Sep 27   Tottenham .... (a)   0-0
(37,092)

Oct 4   Manchester City .... (h)   2-3
(Ball, Cropley; 24,928)

Oct 11   Coventry .... (h)   5-0
(Cropley 2, Ball, Kidd 2; 19,234)

Oct 18   Manchester United ...... (a)   1-3
(Kelly; 52,958)

Oct 25   Middlesbrough .... (h)   2-1
(Stapleton, Cropley; 23,591)

Nov 1   Newcastle .... (a)   0-2
(32,824)

Nov 8   Derby .... (h)   0-1
(32,012)

Nov 15   Birmingham .... (a)   1-3
(Ball; 21,652)

Nov 22   Manchester United ...... (h)   3-1
(Ball, Greenhoff og, Armstrong; 40,102)

Nov 29   West Ham .... (a)   0-1
(31,012)

Dec 2   Liverpool .... (a)   2-2
(Ball pen, Kidd; 27,447)

Dec 6   Leeds .... (h)   1-2
(Brady; 36,003)

Dec 13   Stoke .... (a)   1-2
(Armstrong; 18,628)

Dec 20   Burnley .... (h)   1-0
(Radford; 16,459)

Dec 26   Ipswich .... (a)   0-2
(28,457)

Dec 27   QPR .... (h)   2-0
(Ball, Kidd; 39,021)

Jan 10   Aston Villa .... (h)   0-0
(24,501)

Jan 17   Leicester .... (a)   1-2
(Ross; 21,331)

Jan 31   Sheffield United .... (h)   1-0
(Brady; 14,447)

Feb 7   Norwich .... (a)   1-3
(Kidd; 23,038)

Feb 18   Derby .... (a)   0-2
(24,875)

Feb 21   Birmingham .... (h)   1-0
(Brady; 20,907)

Feb 24   Liverpool .... (h)   1-0
(Radford; 36,127)

Feb 28   Middlesbrough .... (a)   1-0
(Radford; 20,000)

Mar 13   Coventry .... (a)   1-1
(Powling; 13,938)

Mar 16   Newcastle .... (h)   0-0
(18,424)

Mar 20   West Ham .... (h)   6-1
(Ball 2 (1 pen), Armstrong, Kidd 3; 34,011)

Mar 27   Leeds .... (a)   0-3
(26,657)

Apr 3   Tottenham .... (h)   0-2
(42,134)

Apr 10   Everton .... (a)   0-0
(20,774)

Apr 13   Wolves .... (h)   2-1
(Brady, Mancini; 19,518)

Apr 17   Ipswich .... (h)   1-2
(Stapleton; 26,973)

Apr 19   QPR .... (a)   1-2
(Kidd; 30,362)

Apr 24   Manchester City .... (a)   1-3
(Armstrong; 31,003)

Final League Record

P	W	D	L	F	A	Pts	Pos
42	13	10	19	47	53	36	17th

Football League Goalscorers: Kidd 11, Ball 9, Brady 5, Stapleton 4, Cropley 4, Armstrong 4, Radford 3, Kelly 2, Rice 1, Ross 1, Powling 1, Mancini 1, own goal 1

Brian Kidd shoots but Leicester's Wallington saved his effort, September 1975.

1976-7

Bertie Mee had led the Gunners to the supreme 'Double' in 1971 as well as the Fairs Cup the previous season and two League Cup Finals before that. Now the side appeared to have run out of steam and a new face was needed to revitalise and motivate the Arsenal team. The club did not have to look far for a successor — and again he was a man who had spent many happy years at Highbury. Terry Neill, eleven years a Gunner and until a few days previously, manager of neighbours Tottenham, became Arsenal manager in July 1976. A few days later his assistant at White Hart Lane, Wilf Dixon, also moved over. And Neill was soon putting his convictions to the test of public scrutiny. Before he had been at Highbury one month, Neill had broken Arsenal's transfer record by paying Newcastle United £333,333 for striker Malcolm Macdonald. Newcastle's Gordon Lee later said, 'I wouldn't have paid £100,000 — Macdonald's not worth it.' But how wrong he was soon to be proved. Macdonald scored his first goals for Arsenal in a friendly in Switzerland and his first League goal came in the second match of the season when Arsenal made up for an opening day defeat at Bristol City by winning 3-1 at Norwich.

And that was how Macdonald went on for the rest of the season. He scored twenty-five League goals, including hat-tricks against his old club Newcastle and against Birmingham at St Andrew's. Frank Stapleton, no doubt benefiting from the big striker's presence, weighed in with thirteen goals and had now established himself well on the way to becoming one of the First Division's most consistent scorers over the next five years. The Gunners were rarely out of the top-half of the table and although final position of eighth place was not good by Arsenal standards, it was a big improvement on the previous year. The recovery had started.

Players came and went. In September Eddie Kelly signed for QPR for £60,000 and Alex Cropley went to Villa for £125,000, while Terry Mancini was signed by Aldershot. In the same month Newcastle's Pat Howard joined Macdonald at Highbury for £50,000. Before Christmas Alan Hudson was signed from Stoke for £200,000; and Radford went to West Ham (£80,000) and Ball to Southampton (£60,000). One man who wanted to leave but was refused a move was George Armstrong and for a time there was a certain amount of trouble around the affair. Then

Jimmy Rimmer asked for a move but was told he could not go until Neill had found a replacement. In March Willie Young came from Spurs for £80,000 and a day later the unhappy Storey moved to Fulham for £10,000.

Two behind-the-scenes changes were also made. In February, chief scout Gordon Clark left the club, saying he was unable to work with Neill; and at the end of the month that great Arsenal servant Bob Wall retired as general manager. After forty-nine years service to Arsenal, Mr Wall was offered a seat on the Board of Directors which he accepted.

Apart from the low of February and March — when Arsenal broke a fifty-two-year-old record of six consecutive defeats ('We couldn't beat eleven dustbins!' said Terry Neill after a 3-0 defeat at Middlesbrough) and the sending off of Brady at Stoke — Arsenal's side looked to have turned a corner. And for new-signing Macdonald there was a special place in the record books. His hat-trick against Birmingham on 18 January was equalled by one from Francis. Not since 1964 had two players from opposite sides scored hat-tricks in the same First Division match.

Malcolm Macdonald celebrates after scoring Arsenal's third goal against Manchester United, December 1976.

First Division results 1976-7

Aug 21 Bristol City .... (h) 0-1
(41,082)
Aug 25 Norwich .... (a) 3-1
(Nelson. Macdonald, Stapleton; 26,749)
Aug 28 Sunderland .... (a) 2-2
(Ross, Macdonald; 41,211)
Sep 4 Manchester City .... (h) 0-0
(35,132)
Sep 11 West Ham .... (a) 2-0
(Stapleton, Ross; 31,965)
Sep 18 Everton .... (h) 3-1
(Brady, Stapleton, Macdonald; 34,076)
Sep 25 Ipswich.............. (a) 1-3
(Hunter og; 25,505)
Oct 2 QPR .... (h) 3-2
(Rice, Brady, Stapleton; 39,442)
Oct 16 Stoke .... (h) 2-0
(Rice, Macdonald; 28,507)
Oct 20 Aston Villa........... (a) 1-5
(Ball; 33,860)
Oct 23 Leicester............. (a) 1-4
(Stapleton; 19,351)
Oct 30 Leeds .... (a) 1-2
(Matthews; 33,556)
Nov 6 Birmingham........... (h) 4-0
(Stapleton, Ross, Nelson, Macdonald pen;
23,603)
Nov 20 Liverpool .... (h) 1-1
(Armstrong; 45,016)
Nov 27 Coventry .... (a) 2-1
(Macdonald, Stapleton; 18,262)
Dec 4 Newcastle............. (h) 5-3
(Ross, Macdonald 3, Stapleton; 34,053)
Dec 15 Derby .... (a) 0-0
(24,016)
Dec 18 Manchester United ...... (h) 3-1
(Macdonald 2, Brady; 39,572)
Dec 27 Tottenham............ (a) 2-2
(Macdonald 2; 47,751)
Jan 3 Leeds .... (h) 1-1
(Macdonald; 44,090)
Jan 15 Norwich .... (h) 1-0
(Rice; 30,537)
Jan 18 Birmingham........... (a) 3-3
(Macdonald 3; 23,247)
Jan 22 Bristol City .... (a) 0-1
(26,282)

Feb 5 Sunderland .... (h) 0-0
(30,925)
Feb 12 Manchester City .... (a) 0-1
(45,368)
Feb 15 Middlesbrough .... (a) 0-3
(26,000)
Feb 19 West Ham .... (h) 2-3
(Brady, Stapleton; 38,221)
Mar 1 Everton .... (a) 1-2
(Macdonald; 29,802)
Mar 5 Ipswich.............. (h) 1-4
(Macdonald pen; 34,688)
Mar 8 West Brom............ (h) 1-2
(Macdonald; 19,517)
Mar 12 QPR .... (a) 1-2
(Young; 26,191)
Mar 23 Stoke .... (a) 1-1
(Price; 13,951)
Apr 2 Leicester............. (h) 3-0
(Rix, O'Leary 2; 23,013)
Apr 9 West Brom............ (a) 2-0
(Stapleton, Macdonald; 24,275)
Apr 11 Tottenham............ (h) 1-0
(Macdonald; 47,296)
Apr 16 Liverpool .... (a) 0-2
(48,176)
Apr 23 Coventry .... (h) 2-0
(Stapleton, Macdonald; 22,790)
Apr 25 Aston Villa........... (h) 3-0
(Macdonald, Armstrong, Nelson; 23,961)
Apr 30 Newcastle............. (a) 2-0
(Macdonald, Matthews; 44,763)
May 3 Derby .... (h) 0-0
(26,659)
May 7 Middlesbrough .... (h) 1-1
(Stapleton; 23,911)
May 14 Manchester United ...... (a) 2-3
(Brady, Stapleton; 53,232)

Final League Record

P	W	D	L	F	A	Pts	Pos
42	16	11	15	64	59	43	8th

Football League Goalscorers: Macdonald 25, Stapleton 13, Brady 5, Ross 4, Nelson 3, Rice 3, Armstrong 2, O'Leary 2, Matthews 2, Ball 1, Young 1, Price 1, Rix 1, own goal 1

An airborne battle between John Radford and Bristol City's Gary Collier at Highbury, August 1976.

FA Cup

Jan 8 (Rnd 3) Notts County .. (a) 1-0
(Ross; 17,328)
Jan 29 (Rnd 4) Coventry ..... (h) 3-1
(Stapleton, Macdonald 2; 41,078)
Feb 26 (Rnd 5) Middlesbrough . (a) 1-4
(Macdonald; 35,208)
FA Cup Goalscorers: Macdonald 3, Stapleton 1, Ross 1

Football League Cup

Aug 31 (Rnd 2) Carlisle .... (h) 3-2
(Macdonald, Ross 2; 21,550)
Sep 21 (Rnd 3) Blackpool ..... (a) 1-1
(Armstrong; 18,883)
Sep 28 (replay) Blackpool ..... (h) 0-0
(27,165)
Oct 8 (replay) Blackpool ..... (h) 2-0
(Stapleton, O'Leary; 26,791)
Oct 26 (Rnd 4) Chelsea .... (h) 2-1
(Ross, Stapleton; 52,305)
Dec 1 (Rnd 5) QPR......... (a) 1-2
(Stapleton; 27,621)
Football League Cup Goalscorers: Stapleton 3, Ross 3, Macdonald 1, O'Leary 1, Armstrong 1

1977-8

Before the season started Arsenal had released Jimmy Rimmer, who moved to Villa, re-signed Bob Wilson to stand by in case of emergency, and brought off the goalkeeping coup of the decade by signing Spurs' darling Pat Jennings from nearby White Hart Lane for £45,000. Jennings had expressed a desire to stay in the First Division after Spurs were relegated and after talks with Ipswich and Arsenal the brilliant Irishman settled for the Gunners — much to the chagrin of Spurs fans! One move which did not come off was that of Dave Sexton moving to Arsenal as coach. Instead he went to manage Manchester United. Don Howe — Mee's right-hand man in the 'Double' days — then returned to Highbury and Arsenal's talented young team looked set.

Macdonald and Hudson went on the transfer list after being sent home from the Far East tour for 'disciplinary reasons', although Mac soon came off the list and Hudson, though he vowed never to kick another ball for the club, found himself playing for Arsenal in the FA Cup Final later that season! Howard was sold to Birmingham for £35,000 and Arsenal used the money to buy Mark Heeley, Peterborough's young star, for £50,000. As Arsenal progressed to fifth place in the table — they were never out of the top six after November — more transfer deals were set up. On the last day of October Ross moved to Everton

for £170,000; and the following day Wolves' Alan Sunderland came south for £240,000. Wilson's possible comeback had been ruined by a broken wrist, and on 12 November, Macdonald was sent off against Coventry.

But it was the FA Cup which occupied Arsenal's thoughts for the latter half of the season. In the fourth round Macdonald's last-minute goal knocked out Wolves at Highbury and then Walsall were hammered 4-1 to finally lay that ghost of 1933. Wrexham proved no giantkillers in the quarter-finals. And at Stamford Bridge the Gunners easily beat Orient 3-0 to reach their ninth FA Cup Final where they met Ipswich Town, playing in their first. Arsenal were the favourites — but how often the form book has been turned upside-down.

Before the game Bobby Robson told his Ipswich players: 'Stop Nelson and you stop Arsenal!' Ipswich did just that. David Geddis was pulled out

> *Arsenal's 1978 FA Cup final team was: Jennings, Rice, Nelson, Price, O'Leary, Young, Brady (sub Rix), Sunderland, Macdonald, Stapleton, Hudson.*

Frank Stapleton tries a shot at the Ipswich goal during the 1978 FA Cup final.

First Division results 1977-8

Aug 20 Ipswich .... (a) 0-1
(30,173)

Aug 23 Everton .... (h) 1-0
(Powling; 32,954)

Aug 27 Wolves .... (a) 1-1
(Powling; 22,909)

Sep 3 Nottingham Forest ...... (h) 3-0
(Stapleton 2, Brady pen; 40,810)

Sep 10 Aston Villa............ (a) 0-1
(36,929)

Sep 17 Leicester.............. (h) 2-1
(Stapleton, Macdonald; 27,371)

Sep 24 Norwich .... (a) 0-1
(19,312)

Oct 1 West Ham .... (h) 3-0
(Stapleton Rice, Brady pen; 41,245)

Oct 4 Liverpool .... (h) 0-0
(47,110)

Oct 8 Manchester City .... (a) 1-2
(Macdonald; 43,177)

Oct 15 QPR .... (h) 1-0
(Macdonald; 36,172)

Oct 22 Bristol City .... (a) 2-0
(Rix, Macdonald; 25,479)

Oct 29 Birmingham........... (h) 1-1
(Rice; 31,355)

Nov 5 Manchester United ...... (a) 2-1
(Macdonald, Stapleton; 53,055)

Nov 12 Coventry .... (h) 1-1
(Coop og; 31,653)

Nov 19 Newcastle............. (a) 2-1
(Stapleton Sunderland; 22,880)

Nov 26 Derby .... (h) 1-3
(Nelson; 31,939)

Dec 3 Middlesbrough .... (a) 1-0
(Cooper og; 17,422)

Dec 10 Leeds .... (h) 1-1
(Young; 40,162)

Dec 17 Coventry .... (a) 2-1
(Stapleton 2; 21,000)

Dec 26 Chelsea............... (h) 3-0
(Rice, Rix, O'Leary; 46,074)

Dec 27 West Brom............ (a) 3-1
(Sunderland, Macdonald, Brady pen; 27,723)

Dec 31 Everton .... (a) 0-2
(47,039)

Jan 2 Ipswich.............. (h) 1-0
(Price; 43,705)

Jan 14 Wolves .... (h) 3-1
(Brady, Macdonald, Stapleton; 34,784)

Jan 21 Nottingham Forest ...... (a) 0-2
(35,743)

Feb 4 Aston Villa............ (h) 0-1
(30,127)

Feb 11 Leicester............. (a) 1-1
(Brady pen; 15,780)

Feb 25 West Ham .... (a) 2-2
(Macdonald 2; 31,675)

Feb 28 Norwich .... (h) 0-0
(23,506)

Mar 4 Manchester City .... (h) 3-0
(Sunderland, Price, Young; 34,003)

Mar 18 Bristol City .... (h) 4-1
(Stapleton 2, Sunderland, Price; 28,463)

Mar 21 Birmingham........... (a) 1-1
(Brady pen; 22,087)

Mar 25 West Brom............ (h) 4-0
(Macdonald 3 Young; 36,763)

Mar 27 Chelsea............... (a) 0-0
(40,764)

Apr 1 Manchester United ...... (h) 3-1
(Macdonald 2, Brady; 40,739)

Apr 11 QPR .... (a) 1-2
(Brady pen; 25,683)

Apr 15 Newcastle............. (h) 2-1
(Brady, Price; 33,353)

Apr 22 Leeds .... (a) 3-1
(Stapleton, Hart og, Macdonald; 33,263)

Apr 25 Liverpool .... (a) 0-1
(38,318)

Apr 29 Middlesbrough .... (h) 1-0
(Stapleton; 32,238)

May 9 Derby .... (a) 0-3
(21,189)

Final League Record

P	W	D	L	F	A	Pts	Pos
42	21	10	11	60	37	52	5th

Football League Goalscorers: Macdonald 15, Stapleton 13, Brady 9, Price 5, Sunderland 4, Young 3, Powling 2, Rice 2, Rix 2, Nelson, O'Leary 1, own goals 3

A great header by Willie Young is saved by Leicester's Mark Wallington at Highbury, September 1977.

FA Cup

Jan 7   (Rnd 3)   Sheffield United   (a)   5-0
(O'Leary, Macdonald 2, Stapleton 2; 32,156)
Jan 28   (Rnd 4)   Wolves . . . .   (h)   2-1
(Sunderland, Macdonald 49,373)
Feb 18   (Rnd 5)   Walsall . . . .   (h)   4-1
(Stapleton 2, Macdonald, Sunderland; 43,736)
Mar 11   (Rnd 6)   Wrexham . . . . .   (a)   3-1
(Macdonald, Sunderland, Young; 25,500)
Apr 8   (SF)   Orient . . . .   (n)   3-0
(Macdonald 2, Rix; 49,098)
May 6   (Final)   Ipswich . . . .   (W)   0-1
(100,000)

FA Cup Goalscorers: Macdonald 7, Stapleton 4, Sunderland 3, O'Leary 1, Young 1, Rix 1

Football League Cup

Aug 30   (Rnd 2)   Man United . . . .   (h)   3-2
(Macdonald 2, Brady; 36,161)
Oct 25   (Rnd 3)   Southampton . .   (h)   2-0
(Brady pen, Stapleton; 40,749)
Nov 29   (Rnd 4)   Hull City . . . . . .   (h)   5-1
(Brady, Stapleton, Macdonald, Matthews 2; 25,922)
Jan 18   (Rnd 5)   Manchester City   (a)   0-0
(42,000)
Jan 24   (replay)   Manchester City   (h)   1-0
(Brady; 57,748)
Feb 7   (SF, 1st leg)   Liverpool . .   (a)   1-2
(Macdonald; 44,764)
Feb 14   (SF, 2nd leg)   Liverpool .   (h)   0-0
(49,561)

Football League Cup Goalscorers: Macdonald 4, Brady 4, Stapleton 2, Matthews 2

of the middle to harrass the full-back whenever he moved forward with the ball to begin the Gunners' raids. Although Arsenal might have scored when David O'Leary went close, Ipswich's scheme worked like a dream. Paul Mariner sent a shot whistling past Jennings's post and then crashed another against the woodwork. Nelson was forced back and Arsenal's midfield trio were blunted. Up front the Gunners found Allan Hunter and Kevin Beattie were more than a match for their infrequent raids. But still the Suffolk club could not find the net and when John Wark crashed two shots against Arsenal's post, and then Jennings made a wondrous save from George Burley, Bobby Robson must have wondered if his side would ever score. But the goal came. In the seventy-seventh minute Geddis went past Nelson and Hudson and drove a low cross into the goalmouth where Roger Osborne was waiting to slam home the only goal of the game. It was all too much for the Ipswich player who passed out, and was replaced by Mick Lambert. On the day Ipswich deserved to take the Cup. But Arsenal would be back.

Roger Osborne's memorable winner for Ipswich against Arsenal in the 1978 FA Cup final.

1978-9

Arsenal's fifth place in the First Division the previous season gave them a taste of European soccer in the UEFA Cup. But the 1978-9 season will be remembered at Highbury most of all for the club's tenth FA Cup Final appearance—and their fifth win. Certainly no one will want to recall the gloomy night that Third Division Rotherham United knocked them out of the Football League Cup!

Arsenal began the season without the veteran Peter Simpson who left in April 1978 after around 400 games for the Gunners. New understudy goalkeeper was Paul Barron, signed from Plymouth for £70,000, while John Matthews was an early season departure to Sheffield United for £90,000. In October Alan Hudson linked up with North American Soccer League side, Seattle Sounders, thus his last game in an Arsenal shirt was in the FA Cup Final. Young Steve Walford, signed from Spurs a year earlier, made a big impression on the side with twenty-six games plus seven appearances as a substitute. But the big signing of the season was that of Ipswich Town's midfielder, Brian Talbot, who came to Highbury in January for £450,000 and made history by becoming the first player to appear in successive FA Cup-winning teams with different clubs, and then playing in a third final the following year.

> *The team which won the 1979 FA Cup for Arsenal was: Jennings, Rice, Nelson, Talbot, O'Leary, Young, Brady, Sunderland, Stapleton, Price (sub Walford), Rix.*

Macdonald missed most of the season through injury and Frank Stapleton took over as leading scorer with seventeen goals (including his first hat-trick for the club) as Arsenal finished in sixth place. Liam Brady was voted Player of the Year by his fellow professionals to cap another fine season, although it was slightly tarnished when he was sent off in the UEFA tie Hajduk Split at Highbury. In the UEFA Cup Arsenal went out to Red Star Belgrade. After losing only 1-0 in Belgrade the Gunners could only draw at home.

But the FA Cup was still there for the taking and Arsenal played an incredible *five* matches with Sheffield Wednesday before the tie was settled after three replays at Leicester. The two Nottingham clubs went next and Southampton forced a quarter-final replay before Sunderland's two goals saw Arsenal through. Second-half goals against Wolves at Villa Park put Arsenal into the 1979 FA Cup Final and a match against Manchester United, managed by Dave Sexton, the man who was once in line for the Arsenal coaching job.

What a dramatic final it was. Talbot and Stapleton powered the Gunners into a 2-0 half-time lead and with four minutes remaining, Arsenal's colours were being tied to the Cup when McQueen pulled back a goal. Then with only two minutes to play, Sammy McIlroy equalised. There were fantastic scenes and United settled back waiting for the formality of extra-time. But the Cup was not lost to Arsenal yet! In the dying seconds of the game Brady and Rix set up an at-

Brian Talbot puts Arsenal ahead in the 1979 FA Cup final.

Frank Stapleton makes it 2-0 at Wembley.

tack down the left and there was Sunderland to put the ball away. A game which had been fairly unmemorable until the last four minutes would live on in everyone's memory thanks to those dramatic death throes.

FA Cup

Jan 6   (Rnd 3)   Sheffield Wed ..   (a)   1-1
(Sunderland; 33,635)
Jan 9   (replay)   Sheffield Wed .   (h)   1-1
(Brady; 37,987)
Jan 15   (replay)   Sheffield Wed .   (n)   2-2
(Brady, Sunderland; 25,011)
Jan 17   (replay)   Sheffield Wed .   (n)   3-3
(Stapleton 2; Young; 17,008)
Jan 22   (replay)   Sheffield Wed .   (n)   2-0
(Gatting, Stapleton; 30,275)
Jan 27   (Rnd 4)   Notts County ..   (h)   2-0
(Young, Talbot; 39,173)
Feb 26   (Rnd 5)   Nott'm Forest ..   (a)   1-0
(Stapleton; 35,906)
Mar 19   (Rnd 6)   Southampton ..   (a)   1-1
(Price; 24,536)
Mar 21   (replay)   Southampton ..   (h)   2-0
(Sunderland 2; 44,820)
Mar 31   (SF)   Wolves ....   (n)   2-0
(Sunderland, Stapleton; 46,244)
May 12   (Final)   Man United ....   (W)   3-2
(Talbot, Stapleton, Sunderland; 100,000)

FA Cup Goalscorers: Sunderland 6, Stapleton 6, Talbot 2, Brady 2, Young 2, Price 1, Gatting 1

Football League Cup

Aug 29   (Rnd 2)   Rotherham......   (a)   1-3
(Stapleton; 10,481)

Football League Cup Goalscorer: Stapleton

UEFA Cup

Sep 13   (Rnd 1, 1st leg)
         Lokomotive Leipzig .....   (h)   3-0
(Stapleton 2, Sunderland; 34,233)
Sep 27   (Rnd 1, 2nd leg)
         Lokomotive Leipzig .....   (a)   4-1
(Brady, Stapleton 2, Sunderland; 22,000)
Oct 18   (Rnd 2, 1st leg)
         Hajduk Split ....   (a)   1-2
(Brady; 30,000)
Nov 1   (Rnd 2, 2nd leg)
         Hajduk Split ....   (h)   1-0
(Young; 41,787)
Nov 22   Rnd 3, 1st leg
         Red Star Belgrade ....   (a)   0-1
(50,000)
Dec 6   (Rnd 3, 2nd leg)
         Red Star Belgrade ....   (h)   1-1
(Sunderland; 41,566)

UEFA Cup Goalscorers: Stapleton 4, Sunderland 3, Brady 2, Young 1

Alan Sunderland's sensational last-ditch winner brings the FA Cup to Highbury.

First Division results 1978-9

Aug 19   Leeds ....   (h)   2-2
(Brady 2 (1 pen); 42,057)
Aug 22   Manchester City ....   (a)   1-1
(Macdonald; 39,506)
Aug 26   Everton ....   (a)   0-1
(41,179)
Sep 2   QPR ....   (h)   5-1
(Rix 2; Brady, Stapleton 2; 33,474)
Sep 9   Nottingham Forest ......   (a)   1-2
(Brady; 28,124)
Sep 16   Bolton ....   (h)   1-0
(Stapleton; 31,024)
Sep 23   Manchester United ......   (h)   1-1
(Price; 45,393)
Sep 30   Middlesbrough ....   (a)   3-2
(O'Leary, Price, Walford; 14,404)
Oct 7   Aston Villa............   (h)   1-0
(Sunderland; 34,537)
Oct 14   Wolves ....   (a)   0-1
(19,664)
Oct 21   Southampton..........   (h)   1-0
(Brady; 34,074)
Oct 28   Bristol City ....   (a)   3-1
(Brady 2 (1 pen), Stapleton; 27,016)
Nov 4   Ipswich ....   (h)   4-1
(Stapleton 3, Nelson; 35,269)
Nov 11   Leeds ....   (a)   1-0
(Gatting; 33,961)
Nov 18   Everton ....   (h)   2-2
(Brady 2 (1 pen); 39,801)
Nov 25   Coventry ....   (a)   1-1
(Stapleton; 26,786)
Dec 2   Liverpool ....   (h)   1-0
(Price; 51,902)
Dec 9   Norwich ....   (a)   0-0
(20,165)

Dec 16   Derby ....   (h)   2-0
(Price, Stapleton; 26,943)
Dec 23   Tottenham ....   (a)   5-0
(Sunderland 3, Stapleton, Brady; 42,073)
Dec 26   West Brom ....   (h)   1-2
(Brady pen; 40,055)
Dec 30   Birmingham...........   (h)   3-1
(Stapleton, Rice, Sunderland; 27,877)
Jan 13   Nottingham Forest ......   (h)   2-1
(Price, Stapleton; 52,158)
Feb 3   Manchester United ......   (a)   2-0
(Sunderland 2; 45,460)
Feb 10   Middlesbrough ....   (h)   0-0
(28,371)
Feb 13   QPR ....   (a)   2-1
(Price, Brady; 21,125)
Feb 24   Wolves ....   (h)   0-1
(32,215)
Mar 3   Southampton..........   (a)   0-2
(25,052)
Mar 10   Bristol City ....   (h)   2-0
(Rix, Stapleton; 24,408)
Mar 17   Ipswich..............   (a)   0-2
(26,407)
Mar 24   Manchester City ....   (h)   1-1
(Sunderland; 35,014)
Mar 26   Bolton ....   (a)   2-4
(Price, Heeley; 20,704)
Apr 3   Coventry ....   (h)   1-1
(Nelson; 30,091)
Apr 7   Liverpool ....   (a)   0-3
(47,297)
Apr 10   Tottenham ....   (h)   1-0
(Stapleton; 54,041)
Apr 14   West Brom ....   (a)   1-1
(Brady; 28,353)
Apr 16   Chelsea..............   (h)   5-2
(O'Leary, Stapleton 2, Sunderland, Price;
37,232)
Apr 21   Derby ....   (a)   0-2
(18,674)
Apr 25   Aston Villa.............   (a)   1-5
(Stapleton; 26,168)
Apr 28   Norwich ....   (h)   1-1
(Walford; 28,885)
May 5   Birmingham...........   (a)   0-0
(14,015)
May 14   Chelsea..............   (a)   1-1
(Macdonald; 28,386)

Final League Record

P	W	D	L	F	A	Pts	Pos
42	17	14	11	61	48	48	7th

Football League Goalscorers: Stapleton 17, Brady 13, Sunderland 9, Price 8, Rix 3, Macdonald 2, Nelson 2, O'Leary 2, Walford 2, Gatting 1, Rice 1, Heeley 1

1979-80

Arsenal reached their third FA Cup Final in three years and their eleventh in all to equal Newcastle United's record. In addition the Gunners went through to the final of the European Cup-winners' Cup before losing on penalties to the Spanish Cup holders, Valencia. The First Division title was never within the side's grasp, although from 24 November they were never out of the top four, and in the League Cup the Gunners went through to the quarter-finals before Swindon beat them in Wiltshire after an extra-time replay in which seven goals were scored.

Before the season began, Malcolm Macdonald announced his retirement after scoring forty-two goals for Arsenal in eighty-four games—a good striking rate in present-day soccer. But one old name who was about to find a new career at Highbury was John Hollins. The former Chelsea midfielder joined the Gunners from Queens Park Rangers in July and in his first season at the club played in thirty-four League and Cup games, as well as seven appearances as substitute. Hollins's first serious game in an Arsenal shirt was at Wembley on 11 August when the club played League Champions Liverpool in the FA Charity Shield. Arsenal had won the trophy seven times previously but at Wembley that day the Merseysiders played great football and took the Shield 3-1.

Arsenal's League Cup run came to an end in Swindon when own goals from Walford and Hollins gave the home sided a 3-3 draw after ninety minutes. In the 116th minute of the tie Andy Rowlands banged home the winner to leave Arsenal contemplating the fact that Swindon

Brian Talbot's header finally ends the FA Cup semi-final marathon against Liverpool.

Town were something of a bogey side! The UEFA Cup and the FA Cup proved happier hunting grounds. In the European trophy Arsenal went through to the final after a magnificent 1-0 win in Turin against Juventus when substitute Paul Vaessen scored from Rix's cross with only two minutes to play. It was a great win and Arsenal deserved it. In April they played no less than *six* semi-finals—the two legs against Juventus and an amazing four games against Liverpool to decide who should go to Wembley. Eventually, with the FA beginning to wonder if they could stage the final on the proper date, Talbot ended the marathon with a twelfth-minute goal at Coventry in the third replay. A total of 179,163 paid £620,037 to see the four games.

In five days in May Arsenal faced two Cup Finals—and lost them both. On 10 May, against underdogs West Ham, they went down 1-0 to a Trevor Brooking goal to lose the FA Cup to a Second Division club; and in Brussels on 14 May, the Cup-winners' Cup Final went to penalty kicks after 120 minutes had failed to produce a goal. Kempes and Brady missed the first kicks. Then with the score at 4-4 Arias put away Valencia's next shot and Rix's shot was saved by Pereira. Two Cups had been lost in less than a week. Arsenal's only hope of European soccer in 1980-1 was four points from their last two games. They beat Wolves but crashed 5-0 at Middlesbrough. It had been a long, hard season.

Football League Cup

Aug 29 (Rnd 2, 1st leg) Leeds .. (a) 1-1
(Stapleton; 23,421)

Sep 4 (Rnd 2, 2nd leg) Leeds .. (h) 7-0
(Sunderland 3, Nelson, Brady 2 (penalties), Stapleton; 35,129)

Sep 25 Rnd 3) Southampton ... (h) 2-1
(Stapleton, Brady; 34,145)

Oct 30 (Rnd 4) Brighton .... (a) 0-0
(25,231)

Nov 13 (replay) Brighton ...... (h) 4-0
(Stapleton 2, Vaessen 2; 30,351)

Dec 4 (Rnd 5) Swindon ...... (h) 1-1
(Sunderland; 38,024)

Dec 11 (replay) Swindon ...... (a) 3-4
(Brady 2, Talbot; 21,795)

Football League Cup Goalscorers: Stapleton 5, Brady 5, Sunderland 4, Vaessen 2, Nelson 1, Talbot 1

Juventus star Roberto Bettega is tripped by Brian Talbot and the Italian side get a penalty in this European Cup-winners' Cup semi-final first leg at Highbury, April 1980.

First Division results 1979-80

Aug 18   Brighton . . . .   (a)   4-0
(Sunderland 2, Stapleton, Brady pen; 28,604)

Aug 21   Ipswich . . . .   (h)   0-2
(33,245)

Aug 25   Manchester United . . . . . .   (h)   0-0
(44,371)

Sep 1   Leeds . . . .   (a)   1-1
(Nelson; 23,245)

Sep 8   Derby . . . .   (a)   2-3
(Sunderland, Stapleton; 16,429)

Sep 15   Middlesbrough . . . .   (h)   2-0
(Sunderland, Stapleton; 30,341)

Sep 22   Aston Villa . . . .   (a)   0-0
(27,277)

Sep 29   Wolves . . . .   (h)   2-3
(Stapleton, Hollins; 41,844)

Oct 6   Manchester City . . . .   (h)   0-0
(34,688)

Oct 9   Ipswich . . . .   (a)   2-1
(Sunderland, Rix; 21,527)

Oct 13   Bolton . . . .   (a)   0-0
(17,032)

Oct 20   Stoke . . . .   (h)   0-0
(31,591)

Oct 27   Bristol City . . . .   (a)   1-0
(Sunderland; 23,029)

Nov 3   Brighton . . . .   (h)   3-0
(Rix, Brady pen, Sunderland; 34,400)

Nov 10   Crystal Palace . . . .   (a)   0-1
(42,887)

Nov 17   Everton . . . .   (h)   2-0
(Stapleton 2; 33,637)

Nov 24   Liverpool . . . .   (h)   0-0
(55,561)

Dec 1   Nottingham Forest . . . . . .   (a)   1-1
(Stapleton; 27,925)

Dec 8   Coventry . . . .   (h)   3-1
(Stapleton, Sunderland, O'Leary; 27,563)

Dec 15   West Brom . . . .   (a)   2-2
(Nelson, Stapleton; 18,280)

Dec 21   Norwich . . . .   (h)   1-1
(Stapleton; 18,869)

Dec 26   Tottenham . . . .   (h)   1-0
(Sunderland; 48,357)

Dec 29   Manchester United . . . . . .   (a)   0-3
(54,295)

Jan 1   Southampton . . . .   (a)   1-0
(Young; 22,473)

Jan 12   Leeds . . . .   (h)   0-1
(32,799)

Jan 19   Derby . . . .   (h)   2-0
(Brady pen, Young; 22,121)

Feb 9   Aston Villa . . . .   (h)   3-1
(Sunderland 2, Rix; 33,816)

Feb 23   Bolton . . . .   (h)   2-0
(Young, Stapleton; 24,383)

Mar 1   Stoke . . . .   (a)   3-2
(Sunderland, Price, Brady; 19,752)

Mar 11   Bristol City . . . .   (h)   0-0
(21,559)

Mar 15   Manchester City . . . .   (a)   3-0
(Brady 2 (1 pen), Stapleton; 33,792)

Mar 22   Crystal Palace . . . .   (h)   1-1
(Brady; 37,606)

Mar 28   Everton . . . .   (a)   1-0
(Gatting; 28,185)

Apr 2   Norwich . . . .   (a)   1-2
(Rix; 16,923)

Apr 5   Southampton . . . .   (h)   1-1
(Sunderland; 34,593)

Apr 7   Tottenham . . . .   (a)   2-1
(Vaessen, Sunderland; 41,365)

Apr 19   Liverpool . . . .   (a)   1-1
(Talbot; 46,878)

Apr 26   West Brom . . . .   (h)   1-1
(Stapleton; 30,027)

May 3   Coventry . . . .   (a)   1-0
(Vaessen; 16,817)

May 5   Nottingham Forest . . . . . .   (h)   0-0
(34,632)

May 16   Wolves . . . .   (a)   2-1
(Walford, Stapleton; 23,619)

May 19   Middlesbrough . . . .   (a)   0-5
(15,603)

Final League Record

P	W	D	L	F	A	Pts	Pos
42	18	16	8	52	36	52	4th

Football League Goalscorers: Stapleton 14, Sunderland 14, Brady 7, Rix 4, Young 3, Nelson 2, Vaessen 2, Gatting 1, Hollins 1, O'Leary 1, Price 1, Talbot 1, Walford 1

FA Cup

Jan 5 (Rnd 3) Cardiff .... (a) 0-0
(21,972)
Jan 8 (replay) Cardiff .... (h) 2-1
(Sunderland 2; 36,582)
Jan 26 (Rnd 4) Brighton ...... (h) 2-0
(Nelson, Talbot; 43,202)
Feb 16 (Rnd 5) Bolton .... (a) 1-1
(Stapleton; 23,530)
Feb 19 (replay) Bolton .... (h) 3-0
(Sunderland 2, Stapleton; 40,614)
Mar 8 (Rnd 6) Watford ...... (a) 2-1
(Stapleton 2; 28,000)
Apr 12 (SF) Liverpool .... (n) 0-0
(50,174)
Apr 16 (replay) Liverpool ..... (n) 1-1
(Sunderland; 40,679)
Apr 28 (replay) Liverpool ..... (n) 1-1
(Sunderland; 42,975)
May 1 (replay) Liverpool ..... (n) 1-0
(Talbot; 35,335)
May 10 (Final) West Ham ..... (W) 0-1
(100,000)

FA Cup Goalscorers: Sunderland 6, Stapleton 4, Talbot 2, Nelson 1

European Cup-Winners' Cup

Sep 19 (Rnd 1, 1st leg)
Fenerbahce .... (h) 2-0
(Sunderland, Young; 39,973)
Oct 3 (Rnd 1, 2nd leg)
Fenerbahce .... (a) 0-0
(30,000)
Oct 24 (Rnd 2, 1st leg)
Magdeburg .... (h) 2-1
(Young, Sunderland; 34,375)
Nov 7 (Rnd 2, 2nd leg)
Magdeburg .... (a) 2-2
(Price, Brady; 18,000)
Mar 5 Rnd 3, 1st leg
Gothenburg .... (h) 5-1
(Sunderland 2, Price, Brady, Young; 36,323)
Mar 19 (Rnd 3, 2nd leg)
Gothenburg .... (a) 0-0
(40,044)
Apr 9 (SF, 1st leg) Juventus... (h) 1-1
(Bettega og; 51,998)
Apr 23 (SF, 2nd leg) Juventus .. (a) 1-0
(Vaessen; 66,386)
May 14 (Final) Valencia .... (n) 0-0
(40,000) Arsenal lost 4-5 on penalty kicks.

Cup-Winners' Cup Goalscorers: Sunderland 4, Young 3, Price 2, Brady 2, Vaessen 1, own goal 1

> *Arsenal's 1980 FA Cup final side was: Jennings, Rice, Devine (sub Nelson), Talbot, O'Leary, Young, Brady, Sunderland, Stapleton, Price, Rix.*

Trevor Brooking (on ground, white shirt) gives West Ham the FA Cup with a diving header past Pat Jennings in the Arsenal goal.

1980-1

Four Cup Finals in three seasons is in the great traditions of Arsenal Football Club's place at the top of English soccer. And even if three of those games were lost, the fact that the Gunners had reached a hat-trick of FA Cup Finals and played in the Cup-winners' Cup Final, confirmed the status of Terry Neill's side.

Yet European football is the yardstick by which success is measured in the Eighties and the fact remained that Arsenal would not be taking part in any European competition in 1980-1. The Gunners, therefore, had everything to play for in all three domestic competitions in order to re-enter the battlefields of the continent next season. And an opening day win over West Brom at the Hawthorns gave them renewed hope that they would soon be bringing the top sides in Europe back to Highbury.

Even before the season began Arsenal were involved in the mad merry-go-round of football transfers that have spiralled over the last decade. First, star player Liam Brady was transferred to Juventus, the Italian giants, for a comparatively paltry £500,000 when Arsenal had been talking in terms of £1½ million for the player if he went to

Manchester United. Alas, Brady wanted Italian soccer and the European transfer ceiling was well below Arsenal's valuation of their player.

Reaching Cup Finals means making money and Arsenal realised that their profits would be heavily taxed if they did not spend. Within days Clive Allen, Queens Park Rangers striker and son of former Spurs favourite, Les Allen, came to Highbury for £1.2 million—the sixth million-pound player in England. But before he kicked a ball for Arsenal, Allen was on his way to Crystal Palace, together with goalkeeper Paul Barron, while Palace's brilliant young full-back Kenny Sansom came to Highbury with a cash adjustment. It all seemed a bit crazy, but Arsenal had the full-back they wanted and Sansom was a key figure for the rest of the season.

The accompanying statistics show that Arsenal failed in FA Cup and League Cup—and that they almost missed out on a European place, too. But a superb run at the end of the season—hauled the Gunners into third place and into Europe. The last game against Aston Villa saw over 57,000 fans pack Highbury as both sides played for golden rewards—Villa for the title and Arsenal for third place and Europe. Happily, both sides had their reward. Goals by Young, after twelve minutes, and McDermott, after forty-four, gave Arsenal a 2-0 win and that cherished third spot. And Villa took the title as rivals Ipswich crashed at Middlesbrough. Arsenal played the champions off the park and promised to be strong contenders for the title themselves in 1981-2.

John Hollins and Tottenham's Osvaldo Ardiles battle for possession during the First Division match in August 1980. The Gunners won 2-0.

FA Cup
Jan 3   (Rnd 3)   Everton . . . . . .   (a)   0-2
(34,236)

Football League Cup
Aug 26   (Rnd 2, 1st leg)   Swansea .   (a)   1-1
(Stapleton; 17,256)
Sep 2   (Rnd 2, 2nd leg)   Swansea   (h)   3-1
(Hollins, Sunderland, Walford; 26,399)
Sep 22   (Rnd 3)   Stockport . . . . .   (a)   3-1
(Hollins, Sunderland, Stapleton; 11,635)
Nov 4   (Rnd 4)   Tottenham . . . .   (a)   0-1
(42,511)
League Cup Goalscorers: Stapleton 2, Sunderland 2, Hollins 2, Walford 1

First Division results 1980-1

Aug 16   West Brom . . . .   (a)   1-0
(Stapleton; 22,161)

Aug 19   Southampton . . . .   (h)   1-1
(Stapleton; 43,050)

Aug 23   Coventry . . . .   (a)   1-3
(Stapleton; 15,333)

Aug 30   Tottenham . . . .   (h)   2-0
(Price, Stapleton; 54,045)

Sep 6   Manchester City . . . .   (a)   1-1
(Young; 32,233

Sep 13   Stoke . . . .   (h)   2-0
(Hollins, Sanson; 27,183)

Sep 20   Middlesbrough . . . .   (a)   1-2
(Rix; 14,860)

Sep 27   Nottingham Forest . . . . . .   (h)   1-0
(Rix; 37,582)

Oct 4   Leicester . . . .   (h)   1-0
(Stapleton; 28,490)

Oct 7   Birmingham . . . .   (a)   1-3
(Sunderland; 15,511)

Oct 11   Manchester United . . . . . .   (a)   0-0
(49,036)

Oct 18   Sunderland . . . .   (h)   2-2
(Gatting, Young; 32,135)

Oct 21   Norwich . . . .   (h)   3-1
(Talbot, McDermott, Sansom; 21,839)

Oct 25   Liverpool . . . .   (a)   1-1
(Sunderland; 40,310)

Nov 1   Brighton . . . .   (h)   2-0
(Rix, McDermott; 28,569)

Nov 8   Leeds . . . .   (a)   5-0
(Hollins 2, Gatting, Talbot, Sunderland; 20,855)

Nov 11   Southampton . . . .   (a)   1-3
(Rix; 21,234)

Nov 15   West Brom . . . .   (h)   2-2
(Sunderland, Batson og; 25,858)

Nov 22   Everton . . . .   (h)   2-1
(McDermott, Stapleton; 30,911)

Nov 29   Aston Villa . . . .   (a)   1-1
(Talbot; 30,140)

Dec 6   Wolves . . . .   (h)   1-1
(Stapleton; 26,050)

Dec 13   Sunderland . . . .   (a)   0-2
(21,595)

Dec 20   Manchester United . . . . . .   (h)   2-1
(Rix, Vaessen; 33,730)

Dec 26   Crystal Palace . . . .   (a)   2-2
(Stapleton, McDermott; 30,585)

Dec 27   Ipswich . . . .   (h)   1-1
(Sunderland; 42,818)

Jan 10   Everton . . . .   (a)   2-1
(Gatting, Vaessen; 34,236)

Jan 17   Tottenham . . . .   (a)   0-2
(32,994)

Jan 31   Coventry . . . .   (h)   2-2
(Talbot, Stapleton; 24,876)

Feb 7   Stoke . . . .   (a)   1-1
(Stapleton; 14,400)

Feb 21   Nottingham Forest . . . . . .   (a)   1-3
(Stapleton; 25,357)

Feb 24   Manchester City . . . .   (h)   2-0
(Talbot, Sunderland; 24,790)

Feb 28   Middlesbrough . . . .   (h)   2-2
(Stapleton, Hollins; 24,504)

Mar 7   Leicester . . . .   (a)   0-1
(20,198)

Mar 21   Norwich . . . .   (a)   1-1
(Talbot; 19,569)

Mar 28   Liverpool . . . .   (h)   1-0
(Sunderland; 47,058)

Mar 31   Birmingham . . . .   (h)   2-1
(Stapleton, O'Leary; 17,431)

Apr 4   Brighton . . . .   (a)   1-0
(Hollins; 21,015)

Apr 11   Leeds . . . .   (h)   0-0
(29,339)

Apr 18   Ipswich . . . .   (a)   2-0
(Nicholas, Sansom; 30,935)

Apr 20   Crystal Palace . . . .   (h)   3-2
(Talbot, Davis, Young; 24,346)

Apr 25   Wolves . . . .   (a)   2-1
(Berry og, Stapleton; 15,160)

May 2   Aston Villa . . . .   (h)   2-0
(Young, McDermott; 57,472)

Final League Record

P	W	D	L	F	A	Pts	Pos
42	19	15	8	61	45	53	3rd

League Goalscorers: Stapleton 14, Sunderland 7, Talbot 7, Hollins 5, Rix 5, McDermott 5, Young 4, Gatting 3, Sansom 3, Vaessen 2, Price 1, O'Leary 1, Nicholas 1, Davies 1, opponent own goal 2

Brian Talbot's flying header gives Arsenal a goal
against Coventry at Highbury in January 1981.

Ipswich Town's John Wark tries a shot while Willie
Young (No 6) and Brian Talbot (No 4) look on,
December 1980.